Carlyle and the Economics of Terror

Carlyle and the Economics of Terror

A Study of Revisionary Gothicism in The French Revolution

MARY DESAULNIERS

McGill-Queen's University Press
Montreal & Kingston • London • Buffalo

© McGill-Queen's University Press 1995
ISBN 0-7735-1269-1

Legal deposit second quarter 1995
Bibliothèque nationale du Québec

Printed in the United States on acid-free paper

This book has been published with the help of
a grant from the Canadian Federation for the
Humanities, using funds provided by the Social
Sciences and Humanities Research Council of Canada.

McGill-Queen's University Press is grateful to the
Canada Council for support of its publishing
program.

Canadian Cataloguing in Publication Data

Desaulniers, Mary, 1950–
  Carlyle and the economics of terror: a study of
revisionary gothicism in The French Revolution
  Includes bibliographical references and index.
  ISBN 0-7735-1269-1
  1. Carlyle, Thomas, 1795–1881. French Revolution.
  2. Carlyle, Thomas, 1795–1881. – Style. I. Title.
  PR4438.D38 1995   824'.8   C94-900742-0

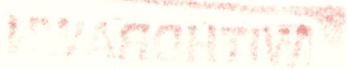

To my best friend, Ed

Contents

Preface ix

Abbreviations x

Introduction 3

1 Carlyle and the Economics of Terror 9

2 Faustian Analogues 34

3 Economics and Economy in *The French Revolution* 60

4 Economics and Economy in the King's Glorious Body 94

5 Afterword: *Sordello* and the Economics of Representation 105

Conclusion 120

Notes 123

Bibliography 129

Index 137

Preface

A preface is an opening statement written at the end when one takes a retrospective pause – a beginning in the end, an end in the beginning. It allows one to reflect on the genesis of the endeavour and to see in the genesis the sources of its inspiration. The reflections that spawned this book came from various sources. I am indebted to a rich and intriguing Carlyle scholarship, particularly that led by Peter Allan Dale, George Levine, Albert J. LaValley, and G.B. Tennyson, who paved the way for a metaphysical encounter with Carlyle's language. To Mark Cumming, I wish to express sincere and heartfelt gratitude, as this book is, in many ways, an offspring of Cumming's *A Disimprisoned Epic*. Two statements made by Cumming in his work helped me define my position. One was Cumming's comment on the "Gothic" nature of *The French Revolution*; the other was his statement on the influence of Carlyle on Browning and the need for further scholarship on the relationship between "brother's speech" in *Sordello* and language in *The French Revolution*. The result is a journey into the implications of Gothicism, economics and language, a journey which places Carlyle within an economy of representation that returns the sign to the materiality of the body. Sign not as metaphysical abstraction, but sign as material incarnation forms the basis of my consideration of "brother's speech" in terms of the incarnational brotherhood of reading.

I wish to thank the members of the Department of English at the University of Western Ontario for their assistance in this project during its early years as a doctoral dissertation. Specific thanks go to my thesis supervisors, Richard Stingle and Donald S. Hair, for their intense support and encouragement through the various stages of the dissertation and its evolution into a book. I wish to thank, as well, several scholars who have provided me with specific recommendations for revisions and publication – Angela Esterhammer, Thomas J. Collins, and John Ferns. As well, I am most grateful to Geoffrey Rans for having enough faith in me to support my return to graduate studies after a thirteen-year hiatus from the academic world.

This book would not have been reality without the continuing support of my companion and soulmate, Ed. Nor would it have been possible without the cooperation of our two children, Jean-Paul and Michael, who suffered joyously through many McDonald and macaroni dinners while the book was in the making.

Quotations from Thomas Carlyle's works are cited in the text using the following abbreviations:

CL *The Collected Letters of Thomas and Jane Welsh Carlyle*, ed. Charles Richard Sanders and Kenneth J. Fielding, 9 vols. (Durham: Duke University Press, 1970–81)
C *The Correspondence of Carlyle and Emerson*, ed. Charles Eliot Norton, 2 vols. (London: Chatto, 1883)
W *The Works of Thomas Carlyle*, Centenary ed., 30 vols. (New York: AMS, 1969)
TNB *Two Note Books of Thomas Carlyle*, ed. Charles Eliot Norton, 1989 (Mamaroneck: Appel, 1972)

References from the first three works are cited to volume and page.

Carlyle and the Economics of Terror

Introduction: Carlyle and the Economy of the Body/Text

In the fall of 1832, a cholera epidemic seized the Dumfries. The casualty rate was high: five hundred souls from a population of thirteen thousands. Panic was widespread, the people succumbing to a "terror" Carlyle felt was "disgraceful" (*CL*, 6:267). In a letter to John Stuart Mill, Carlyle describes the course of the disease as rather "violent," "the people in a shocking panic, so that all communication is obstructed ... The terror of the World at this Pestilence is such as if Death had never been heard of. Nevertheless Death is *not* new; moreover, come when or how it will, it should find us *at our working and thinking mainly of our work*" (*CL*, 6:239). With stoic equanimity, Carlyle refuses to be the victim of terror; he looks Death in the eye: "The sooner we grow to compose ourselves beside it, the wiser for us. A man who has reconciled himself *to die* need not go distracted at the *manner* of his death" (*CL*, 6:244).

Such composed defiance is not unusual for Carlyle, whose letters are filled with acknowledgment of a body in flux, a sick and ailing body which can neither be controlled nor cured, only stoically endured. Implicit in his equanimity is a criticism of the panic-stricken populace, whose terror is evidence of unconscious neglect. They have forgotten the place of death in their lives; they have forgotten the "taste of fear"; their panic is therefore a return of the repressed.

There seems, however, no place for such forgetfulness in the Carlylean body. For a man cursed by a recalcitrant digestive system, tormented by chronic pain and debility, suffering, if not death, is always at the door. Fred Kaplan, in his biography of Carlyle, makes a strong association between his stomach and his temper: "When the 'weary bowels had got cross again,' he felt 'bilious' – weak, tired, self-critical, and despairing."[1] In his letters, Carlyle complains bitterly of an uncooperative stomach, which he feels is caused by "distracted" London. Even though Jane, his wife, prefers the social consolation of the city, Carlyle is adamant about returning to the country. Their move to Craigenputtoch is part of Carlyle's "fantasy that rural life [is] good for his health."[2] One can imagine Carlyle's stubbornness and complaints to be a source of frayed nerves and temper. Jane, who herself suffers a good deal from headaches and weakness, reads Carlyle's malady with typical Scottish acuity. In a letter to her mother-in-law, she writes: "Carlyle keeps saying he is very bilious – &c&c, but he looks very passably [sic], is not so desperately *'ill to deal wi'* as you and I have known him and has always a good 'harl of health at meal time[']" (*CL*, 10:227). By 1839, well after the publication and successful reception of *The French Revolution*, Carlyle is able to perceive that his ailment has a strong psychosomatic component.[3] The severity of his symptoms seems to abate with emerging confidence and faith in himself. But while he seems to be moderately surprised by his more cooperative body, he remains seduced by the "convalescent" mentality that resurfaces with the aggravation of Jane's symptoms. The letters of the Carlyles are replete with references to a disintegrating or almost recovering body.

This preoccupation with health and illness is typical of Carlyle's sensitivity to the world of paradox. Health and illness are not mutually exclusive terms for him; they stand one with the other in a distinctive economy of the body. In a letter to his brother James in 1838, Carlyle makes a wish for perfect health; yet, ten lines later, he rejects this wish: "I think if I were rightly healthy, rightly as in old young days, I should fly out of this world" (*CL*, 10:233–4). He realizes that perfect health means annihilation and unconsciousness (*W*, 28:1) and that while one strives towards perfect health, one can only be self-consciously aware of its impossibility. Jane seems unusually cognizant of the irony implicit in her husband's preoccupation with health. In a letter to Frances Wedgwood, she writes: "[Carlyle] can do much, but he cannot be *impudent* for the life of him: and a vehement longing for *good* health is apt to defeat its object" (*CL*, 10:35).

Carlyle's assimilation of health and illness within an economy of the body is evident in both physical and metaphysical concerns. If the Carlylean body is a site of dissolution and recovery, the Carlylean text is a site of dialectical opposition. Text and body are both *enacted* in a language which attempts to break out of the arbitrary and conventional into some form of linguistic recovery. The "whole" text, like the "whole" body, embraces a necessary doubleness. In his journal of 1831, Carlyle makes a claim for the "wholeness" of Art over Religion; this "wholeness" is defined as a form of doubleness:

When Goethe and Schiller say or insinuate that Art is higher than Religion, do they mean perhaps this: That whereas Religion represents (what is the essence of Truth for men) the Good as *infinitely* (the word is emphatic) different from the Evil, but sets them in a state of *hostility* (as in Heaven and Hell), – Art likewise admits and inculcates this quite infinite difference; but *without* hostility, with peacefulness; like the difference of two Poles which *cannot* coalesce, yet do not quarrel, nay should not quarrel for both are essential to the whole? (*TNB*, 204)

For Carlyle, art transcends the Manichean dualism of Religion by generating wholeness, by cultivating the "quite infinite difference" between Good and Evil, but *"without* hostility." Art demands the prerogative to go beyond the Christian paradigm of good versus evil.

This aesthetic prerogative becomes a Carlylean signature. Because he insists on an authentic doubleness in language, his prose is often labelled "unintelligible," replete with the densely woven structures of a "self-conscious modernity."[4] Resistant and obscure, Carlyle's style has been the bane of every reader who has attempted to come to terms with his works. *The French Revolution* is no exception; indeed this historical epic marks such a wild departure from nineteenth-century literary and historical conventions that John D. Rosenberg refers to its technique as an "incessant dialectic of contraries."[5] Gothic in impetus, revolutionary in form, the stylistic excess of *The French Revolution* remains strong testimony to a nineteenth-century preoccupation with recovering linguistic holism.

Money is the culmination of man's abstraction from a natural and holistic materialism. By insisting on the "symbolization" of value, that logic of exchange by which thing is separated from the abstract value imposed on it, money removes man from a native Imaginary wholeness. Carlyle sees this tropological basis of money as the source of inflationary language. Sundered by the Lockean separation of word and thing, reduced to an instrument of convention and circulation, such language has fallen, in the words of Carlyle, into "Mammonism" which "left to itself, has become Midas-eared," a reference to the Midas wish that left this avaricious king starving in the midst of plenty. Language which fails to feed the soul of man is part of a system that has gone awry: "with all [his] gold mountains," man "sits starving for want of bread" (*W*, 10:195). "England is full of wealth" (*W*, 10:1), yet "a Mother and a Father are arraigned and found guilty of poisoning three of their children, to defraud a 'burial-society' of some [money] due on the death of each child" (*W*, 10:4). Such are the marks of terror in a system that has allowed economics to usurp natural order. Terror, in this sense, is the logical consequence of misplaced faith in economic viability. Terrifying as these events may be, they stand for Carlyle as both "signs of the times" and signs of recovery. "This English Nation, will it get to know the meaning of *its* strange new Today?" (*W*, 10:7). The lesson to be learned from Midas is that he has parted company with "Nature's right truth" (*W*, 10:8). The lesson to be learned from England's terror is that she has moved away from a natural social economy.

A society that rejects Mammonism will place as priority not the production of "cheaper produce exclusively" in the interest of profit but "fairer distribution of the produce at its present cheapness" (*W*, 10:271). The language that emerges from such society will be evidence of a holistic economy (from the word *oikonomia*, which means "management").[6] The poet "who [has] looked merely to reviewers, copyrights, booksellers, popularities" (*W*, 10:205) sees language only in terms of "wages" (*W*, 10:204); he has, in fact, sold his "talent" and reduced infinity to a price. The economy of language demands a more authentic commitment to wholeness, a commitment that goes beyond wages or consensus; hence Carlyle's emphasis on "labour," the god encased in Mammonism and ever struggling to be free: "labour is ever an imprisoned god, writhing unconsciously or consciously to escape out of Mammonism" (*W*, 10:207). Labour is language in a "dialectic of contraries" overthrowing the yoke of consensus for a more legitimate basis of representation. Labour is the "convalescent" body ever conscious of death and struggling towards recovery. Ultimately, labour is the Gothic "terror" that restores the economics of the word to an economy of prophetic holism.

Five areas, each explored in a separate chapter, are seminal to my investigation of revisionary Gothicism in *The French Revolution*. First, Coleridge's distinction between allegory and symbol remains useful in demarcating the boundaries between fallen and redemptive language, inflationary and solvent texts. In assimilating these distinctions within the economy of the word, Carlyle's engagement of transcendental philosophy seems more than passing fancy. His understanding of transcendental philosophy comes mainly from Coleridge, who locates the source of creative power in the "irreconcilable contradiction" of the third term. This third term provides

Carlyle with a prototype of linguistic holism with which to counteract the reductionism of fallen language. While the latter speaks solely from an economic bias, prophetic or holistic language sounds the depth of authentic engagement within the doubled economy of the third term. In the first chapter, I trace the context of money and signs within which this paradigm of economy and economics can be constellated. Kant, Coleridge, and Adam Smith provided me with the necessary lines of demarcation. Carlyle's assimilation of these lines enables him to make *The French Revolution* a deliberate response to Edmund Burke's *Reflections on the Revolution in France*. Burke sees the revolution as an economic collapse, a "shop of horrors."[7] Carlyle, however, urges for a more holistic reading of the crisis, one that would replace Burke's economics of terror with the economy of the event.

In the second chapter, I use a field of precursor texts to establish the conventional lines of Gothicism which Carlyle both sustains and dissolves. Goethe's *Faust* and the German style Gothic romances of Maturin and Lewis remain precursor texts providing narrative lines for Carlyle's deployment of an economics of terror. To the extent that early Gothic romances moved against the logic of "currency," they remain viable to my consideration of language and its resistance to the current flow. The Gothic dissolution of rationalism marks the point at which the text becomes a source of betrayal and it is this betrayal that sustains the necessary "fiction" of language. Goethe's *Faust* provides the blueprint for such "thieving" language.

In the third chapter, I focus exclusively on Carlyle's dilation of economics and representation in *The French Revolution*, bringing in through this dilation a host of subtexts on "reading": the Gothic betrayal of body and text, the economic ramifications of the body politic, the "representational" dynamics of the Eucharist, and the role of the reader as the political body within an "act" of reading. Ultimately the metaphor of reading or misreading becomes a political act of investiture. Reading as an act of constitution is the very problem enacted in Carlyle's revolution. Does the reader stand in symbiotic relationship with the author? Is the reader allowed the grace of re-creation or is he a corollary of the "constituted" text? Is he, like the revolutionaries, betrayed by the "constituted" sign? By collapsing the National Constitution into the Reign of Terror, Carlyle exposes the untenable status of a consensual mandate. The "Constitution," that legacy of community and consensus, remains both a thematic and self-reflexive constituent of the linguistic process. Intrinsic in this process is the "dis-imprisoning" of the word from the "wages" of the arbitrary. The "wagered" word therefore assumes a dimension that develops in *The French Revolution* from a crisis in kingship to a crisis in reading.

In chapter 4, this assimilation of text, body, and politics is aligned with Louis Marin's discussion of the iconic imperative within the "King's Glorious Body." Like Rousseau's *Social Contract*, the King's Glorious Body assumes the dimensions of what Paul de Man calls "metaphorical totalization."[8] If reading puts into question rhetorical patterns of totalization, then language can never be more than a "promise," a contractual wager that promises yet never delivers its goods. De Man's metaphor of (mis)reading provides a seductive paradigm for Carlyle reading Rousseau and for the (mis)reading of the political events of 1780s as generation of history. Ultimately the King's Body becomes a metaphor for the dissolution and unification of the political body. In a parallel way, Carlyle's own language becomes the site at which allegory and symbol are severed and coalesced.

Finally, the economic dimensions of *The French Revolution* are further validated in chapter 5 when the text is seen as precursor to Browning's *Sordello*, whose unfolding of a crisis in kingship and language is strong testimony that the economics of representation remains a pivotal nineteenth-century strategy for a select readership. Carlyle's Gothicism in *The French Revolution* is a strategy for revisioning language. By challenging the "economics" of the word, it validates his position within a nineteenth-century tradition of prophetic language.

1 Carlyle and the Economics of Terror

The place of Carlyle's *The French Revolution* in the context of nineteenth-century narrative tradition is an anomalous one; neither history nor fiction, neither tragedy nor comedy, the work demands an encounter of its own kind. That it stands at a stylistic watershed is evident when Carlyle calls his work "a *queer* book ... one of the *queerest* published in this Century" (*CL*, 8:209). Indeed, Emerson gently reproaches Carlyle for writing a work that is "Gothically efflorescent" and insists that "it might be [made] more simple" (*C*, 1:131). But Carlyle seems wholly committed to the "savagery" of the piece, calling it in mock deprecatory terms a "wild savage ruleless very bad Book" (*CL*, 9:82).

In the years since it was published, however, critics have attempted to tame this savage book. The Gothic nature of *The French Revolution* has generated some interest in current criticism, much of which has focused on either a psychological or a generic exploration of its use. Some critics see Carlyle's Gothicism as part of an inherent psychological necessity. Burton Friedman, for example, claims that Carlylean metaphysics anticipate Freudian psychology.[1] On the other hand, Mark Cumming, in *A Disimprisoned Epic*, sees Carlyle's infernal/supernal evocations as part of his revisionary epic machinery: Gothicism emerges as part of the "phantasmagoria" which explodes into a Copernican repudiation of superannuated forms.

Central to Cumming's comments on Carlyle's "phantasmagoria" is the paradox involved in Carlyle's use of Gothicism. Carlyle's rejection of popular fiction is a well-known fact; his adoption of this popular mode is ironic within the context of this prejudice. A master satirist, Carlyle resurrects Gothic conventions in order to repudiate the very machinery of Gothicism itself. It seems necessary that Carlyle manipulate a "current" style, for his rejection of the Gothic mode stems from a repudiation of a "bastardized" form which has grown too "current" for its own good and from a revisionary accommodation of the original purpose of the genre. Walpole, who christened *The Castle of Otranto* a "gothic" work, maintained that it was written in order to let loose "the great resources of fancy, unfortunately dammed-up by common life."[2] Walpole's original intention was, therefore, to produce a work which moved not with but against the current. However, mass circulation of Gothic fiction had caused the genre to become a repository for literary clichés, especially repugnant to those insistent on "classicism." In "Taylor's Historic Survey of German Literature," Carlyle mocks British "priggishness" towards the "savage" publications of their Gothic neighbours. He quotes Hannah More's injunctions to the ladies of "taste" to "oppose ... the irruption of those swarms of Publications now daily issuing from the banks of the Danube, which, like their ravaging predecessors of the darker ages ... are overrunning civilised society." She asks readers whose "purer taste has been formed on the correct models of the old classic school" to denounce the "Huns and the Vandals" for overpowering the Greek and Roman empires of classicism. Carlyle's view of the "Paper Goths" is more casual: "Like the old Northern Immigrators," he writes, "those new Paper Goths marched on resistless whither they were bound; some to honour, some to dishonour, the most to oblivion and the impalpable inane" (W, 27:334). If the "Gothic" suggests unrestrained energy, its embodiment runs the gamut from the current and sentimental representations of "Bibliopolic profit" (W, 27:337) to the rare, but genuine, articulations of "Primitive Truth" (W, 26:79).

What Carlyle's Gothicism involves, then, is a separation of the current from the genuine, the derivative imitations of a popular form from its more intrinsic and motivated appropriations. In many respects, his Gothicism is a transposition of the Blakean metaphor of "printing in the infernal method, by corrosives ... melting apparent surfaces away, and displaying the infinite which was hid."[3] Indeed, Carlyle's *The French Revolution* is itself an infernal text whose method of production goes beyond Blake's repetitive circulation of intellectual cannibalism, emblemized in the vision of self-ingesting primates,[4] to comprehend, in its wake, a form of corrosive purification – a baptism by fire in order to release the energies by "melting the metals into living fluids."[5]

Both Blake and Carlyle see in Gothic form a viable alternative to language made mechanical by the arbitrary sign. In "State of German Literature," Carlyle describes the "Bread-Artist," the poet who sells his work as a "tradesman [offering] his talent in open market, to do work ... for hire" (W, 26:57). Such exchange of art for public support, like inquiring after the "*utility* of a God" (W, 26:56), is a form of self-ingesting slavery, for the "[merchant] of literature," tempted by the diurnal round of "economic concerns," is made hourly to "sink from an artist into a manufacturer" (W, 26:44). Carlyle's favourite quotation from Schiller delineates the poet as a force, not of profit, but of purification: "let him [the artist] return, a foreign shape, into his century; not however, to delight by his presence, but dreadful, like the Son of Agamemnon, to purify it" (W, 26:57). Again, in "Goethe," Carlyle asserts that poetry cannot be a "superficial, cursory business," the kind that is transparent at a glance, "which may be seen through to the very bottom, so soon as one inclines to cast his eye on it." Such poetry belongs to the "current" kind; it supplies "spouting-clubs" and "circulates in circulating libraries"; such poetry belongs to a species which "has circulated and will circulate and ought to circulate, in all times" (W, 26:255). But such poetry remains speculative: it will never break out of the "round" into prophecy.[6] Carlyle's intentional collation of currency, circulation, and comprehensibility sustains a prejudice against the reductive nature of language in popular art. Here he echoes Schlegel, who in his essay "On Incomprehensibility" mocks the whimsical nature of an art made as accessible as "popular alchemy." To create a comprehensible language is to create a system of signification as arbitrary as currency:

In the nineteenth century, so Girtanner assures us, in the nineteenth century, man will be able to make gold; and isn't it now more than mere conjecture that the nineteenth century is shortly going to begin? With laudable confidence and some huffing and puffing, the working man says: "Every chemist, every artist will make gold; the kitchen utensils are going to be made of silver, of gold." How gladly all artists will now resolve to go on being hungry for the slight insignificant remainder of the eighteenth century and in future no longer fulfill this sacred duty with an aggrieved heart; for they know that ... their descendants will shortly be able to make gold.[7]

This rejection of "popular" language on the basis of its democratic appeal has a strong history in German Enlightenment writing. Carlyle's acceptance of critical philosophy is based almost entirely on its deliberate cultivation of opacity and the concomitant demands this opacity places on the reader. Such darkness, Carlyle claims in

"State of German Literature," is but "transitory obscuration: these ashes are the soil of future herbage and richer harvests" (*W*, 26:85). In his *Prolegomena to Any Future Metaphysics*, Kant similarly criticizes the appeal to common sense which opponents to "pure thinking" often lodge against the "difficulty" of a Kantian text: "it is but an appeal to the opinion of the multitude," writes Kant, "of whose applause the philosopher is ashamed, while the popular charlatan glories and boasts in it."[8] The collation of sound common sense with "counterfeit" or paper currency can be seen in the pervasiveness of "market" metaphors in German Enlightenment discourses. Schiller, in his second Aesthetical Letter, speaks of the "great idol" Utility, worshipped in the "noisy Vanity Fair of our time."[9] Again, in "On the Study of Philosophy," Schelling compares the popular demand for intelligibility to "hard cash": "The understanding which non-philosophy calls sound common sense wants the truth in hard cash, as it were, and tries to get it regardless of the inadequacy of its resources."[10]

What emerges in these denunciations of coins and currency is a critique of the arbitrary sign in a language reduced, like money, to a conventional sign system. In a market economy, dominated by market imperatives, "sheer symbols of exchange are treated as the basic motives of human relations." What this effects is a "'transubstantiation' of money, from its function as an *agency* of economic action into a function as the *ground* or *purpose* of economic action."[11] In short, money as a symbol of exchange becomes literal through use, and economics supplants economy as the motive of exchange. In *The Politics*, Aristotle makes a distinction between proper "economy" (*oikonomia*), the natural and judicious management of a household, and improper "economics" or usury. The former is "necessary and praised, while expertise in exchange is justly blamed since it is not according to nature but involves taking from others." Such usury "is most reasonably hated because one's possessions derive from money itself and not from that from which it was supplied."[12] That which should be understood as a *trope* to facilitate exchange is taken for the *substance* itself: "That is, instead of *using* money as a medium to facilitate the production and distribution of goods, men were moved to produce and distribute goods in response to money as motive."[13]

This assumption of profit as motive is explained by Carlyle as a consequence of the rift between signifier and signified. If Adamic language comprehends a fusion of sign and signified, so that words prophesy in an unconscious and creative fiat, fallen language can only partially articulate this wholeness, for sign disjoined from significance can produce only a "prison-house" of language; the body becomes the "prison-house of the soul," writes Carlyle in "Characteristics," and can participate only in an artificial and mechanical consciousness. The Imaginary wholeness in Adamic language is reproduced in this essay as a healthy form of unconsciousness. "The perfection of bodily well-being," Carlyle asserts, "is that the collective bodily activities seem one; and be manifested, moreover, not in themselves, but in the action they accomplish" (W, 28:1). The semiotic economy of an Imaginary wholeness resides in the "symbiotic" relationship between mother and child; such symbiosis is reproduced in the plenitude of a body in complete health, "each organ [performing] its function, unconsciously, unheeded" (W, 28:1). Language, within the reciprocity of an Imaginary exchange, is "'genius ... ever a secret to itself'" (W, 28:5); intuition, unlike the "little compact theorem of the world" (W, 28:6), is whole but incomprehensible. Only when language enters the Symbolic agency of the understanding does it become separated from itself; in Eagleton's terms, it is "plunged into post-structuralist anxiety."[14] Speculation, emerging from this repression of desire, can never be truly creative; at best, Carlyle claims, it is a language which endeavours "to bring the Phenomena of man's Universe ... under some theoretic Scheme" (W, 28:33); at worst, it becomes a "shameful Abortion," "perhaps absurdest Book written in our century by a thinking man" (W, 28:36). Fallen language, confined to the "outer, thin and barren domain of the Conscious or Mechanical," can never retrieve the "mystery and miracle" of the "inner sanctuaries" (W, 28:40) unless it is purified and made into the motivated language of intuition.

For Carlyle, the "monied interests" of landed property contribute to this "abortion" of language. Jean Paul was not of "monied interests," Carlyle argues in his essay on Richter; "he was not a nobleman, nor gentleman, nor gigman," but "simply a man" (W, 27:130). It is this distinction between a monied man and "simply a man" that is central to Carlyle's distinction between a language dominated by profit motive and a language made vital by "symbiotic" exchange. This distinction is a crucial one, for Carlyle sees in "monied interests" not only a political deployment of wealth and power but a perversion of the elemental economy of man.

In this sense, he discerns the same discrepancy Adam Smith perceives between the "use" or "labour" value and the "exchange" value of a product. In his *Enquiry into the Wealth of Nations*, Smith insists on differentiating between real and nominal prices. Smith locates "real" value in labour and consigns money to a tropological or nominal role. "Labour," he writes, "is the real measure of the exchangeable value of all commodities";[15] but, because "[i]t is more natural ... to estimate [a commodity's] exchangeable value by the quantity of some other commodity than by that of the labour which it can purchase," money became the "common instrument of commerce" (1:36). The displacement of the real price (labour) by the nominal price (money) has resulted in an erroneous association of money with revenue, an association which Smith labours to correct: "though the metal pieces of which it [money] is composed, in the course of their annual circulation, distribute to every man the revenue which properly belongs to him, they make themselves no part of that revenue" (1:309). For Smith, revenue should be equated with the "consumptibility" of goods, not with a third-party term like money. His perception that money is, in effect, an abstraction from material existence is reflected in his persistent references to money as simply "metal pieces" (1:307) that function as "an instrument of commerce" (1:306) or a "wheel of circulation" (1:309). Elsewhere, he insists that the "real" value of money lies not in the money itself, but in what it can purchase (1:306–09).

That money elaborates man's separation from his fundamental nature, that money alienates man from the material conditions of his existence, can be seen in the difference between an exchange made under a barter economy and an exchange made under a money economy. Inherent in the logic of exchange is a doubling of perspectives: the giver and the taker both participate in a form of symbiotic reciprocity. This doubling in a pre-capitalist barter economy is a simple give-and-take transaction. It is what Jean-Joseph Goux in *Symbolic Economies* describes as a "dual maternal signifying economy" characterized by a "reciprocal and contradictory mother-child relationship, prior to the law of the intervening third."[16] In short, for Goux, barter exchange is fraught with the specular dimensions of a Lacanian mirror stage: "One of the commodities expresses its value in the *body* of the other, which thus serves as *matter* (mother, material, matrix) for this expression."[17] Each commodity becomes a material or bodily expression of its specular other. If barter economy is a material body exchange, money economy, an effect of capitalism, can be seen as an immaterially transcendent substitution, one presided over by the "law of the father." Marc Shell, in *The Economy of Literature*, elaborates on this distinction between simple barter and money economies: "In barter economy, one actor gives X to a second actor and this second actor gives Y to the first actor. Marine pastures can be bartered for land pastures. In a barter economy, no commodity (not even gold) attains the status of money ... In a money economy, one thing is not exchanged directly for another, but is exchanged for money which seems to represent or be all things."[18] It is this generation of money as a third or mediating term which distinguishes money economy from simple barter. In *Sartor Resartus*, Carlyle associates the emergence of this "general equivalent" in writing with the emergence of democracy and money economy. He who "[cashiers] ... Kings and Senates and [creates] a whole new Democratic world" also "[invents] the Art of Printing," for the manufacture of words by general consensus as part of an abstracting imperative is as insistent as the abstraction of money from a barter economy: "A simple invention it was in the old-world Grazier ... to take a piece of Leather, and thereon scratch or stamp the mere Figure of an Ox (or *Pecus*); put it in his pocket, and call it *Pecunia*, Money. Yet hereby did Barter grow Sale, the Leather Money is now Golden and Paper, and all miracles have been out-miracled: for there are Rothschilds and English National Debts; and whoso has sixpence is sovereign ... over all men" (W, 1:31). This abstraction of money from the circuit of commodity exchange is the equivalent of self-consciousness in "Characteristics": "let but an organ announce its separate existence, were it even boastfully, and for pleasure, not for pain, then already has one of these unfortunate 'false centres of sensibility' established itself, already is derangement there" (W, 28:1). A money economy is an unnatural derangement of the Adamic word.

Almost forty years after the publication of *Sartor Resartus*, Marx refers to money as a form of "universal prostitution." As "general equivalent," money becomes standard behaviour which can be exchanged without exception: "the exchangeability of all products, activities and relationships against a third, or *material*, factor, which can be exchanged against everything else *without exception* – in other words the development of exchange values (and money relationships) – is the same thing as general venality and corruption".[19] In the interest of "serviceability" and "usefulness," the general equivalent brings "different things to a common level"; this levelling of "personal talents, abilities, capacities and activities" is a necessary prelude to "universal prostitution" (71). The entrance of money into the Symbolic realm demands the sacrifice of differences to the "law of the father," a sacrifice which culminates in the universalizing tendency of money as a third term. The democratic appeal of money becomes, for Marx, the basis of alienated labour. In *Grundrisse*, Marx locates alienation in the "abstraction" which occurs when a product is converted into a commodity, that is, a "pure element of exchange": "When the product becomes a commodity and the commodity becomes exchange value, it possesses (ideally at first) a double existence. This ideal dual identity necessarily means that the commodity appears in a dual form when actually exchanged: as natural product on the one hand, as an exchange value on the other. In other words, its exchange value has a material existence, apart from the product" (59). Thus the perception of a product as exchange value necessarily severs the product's material nature from its tropological one. Money, for example, which begins as a product, becomes itself pure exchange value; society's repeated elaboration of the social form of money has helped dissolve the material basis of money. More commodity than product, its exchange value more detached from its use value, money becomes the most abstracted symbol of alienated society. Marx states that the alienated existence imposed on money by a market imperative inevitably leads to inverted "money relationships": "The more the producers become dependent upon exchange, the more exchange seems to be independent of [them]; and the gap between the product as a product and the product as an exchange value widens" (61). This generation of the "transcendental form of money" becomes the sign of a de-materialized and abstracted culture, for the immediate purpose of trade becomes "not consumption," but the "amassing of money, of exchange values" (63).

It is precisely this aspect of money, as an abstraction from material culture, that informs Carlyle's insistent dissolution of Rousseau's "Social Contract" in *The French Revolution*. Implied in Rousseau's Republic One and Indivisible is the assumption that "community" itself is not an inherent part of natural man; indeed, he becomes communal man only with and through the contract, or, in other words, exchanges the freedom inherent in his animal nature for the "community" of civil society. The Social Contract, as a discourse of exchange, is the very means by which man transcends his animal nature to become a civil being; like money, the Social Contract is an abstracted "general equivalent" which, in its mediating capacity, erases all differences. Rousseau himself intimates the "totalitarian" bias of his Social Contract when he insists that "whoever refuses to obey the general will shall be constrained to do so by the whole body, which means nothing other than that he shall be forced to be free."[20] Carlyle's distrust of such contractarian ideology can be seen in his association of democracy with printing. In "The Hero as a Man of Letters," he collates the dissemination of the printed word with the "popular" imperatives of a democratic process. "Literature," he writes, "is our Parliament too. Printing which comes necessarily out of Writing, I say often, is equivalent to Democracy: invent Writing, Democracy is inevitable. Writing brings Printing, brings universal every-day extempore Printing" (W, 5:164). The contractarian imperatives behind propaganda come to the fore in *The French Revolution* as the circulating, inflationary currency of the "Paper Age." Carlyle's rejection of paper democracy is as much a rejection of paper money: both are displaced substitutes, phantom proxies of the "real thing." Paper currency, in its dissimulation of real gold, is as abominable as a man "[wearing] the clothes and [taking] the wages of ... another" (W, 5:165). In Carlylean economy, the genuine has to be differentiated from the counterfeit, the "false and tawdry ware" (W, 26:31) from genuine gold, which is not a "general equivalent" of abstracted and arbitrary value, but the "everlasting gold of truth" that must be purified from its "ponderous unmanageable dross" (W, 25:114).

For Carlyle, the abstraction implicit in a money economy need not turn into the totalitarian imperative it becomes under capitalism; he counters the universalizing tendency of money to reduce the many to one with the "fitful adumbration of many" (W, 26:196) in transcendental philosophy. Kant's positing of intuition as a third term allows his transcendentalism to go beyond the arbitrary reductionism of popular philosophy. What Carlyle sees in the third term agency of Kant and Schelling is a possible alternative to the abstracting third term in money economy.

To clarify this position, I would like to make a detour to Coleridge who, in chapter 13 of the *Biographia Literaria*, locates what he perceptively concludes to be the key to transcendental philosophy. This key is the nature of mediation embraced by a third-term agency. Summarizing and transposing Kant at the same time, Coleridge focuses on the distinction Kant makes between "logical" and "real" oppositions. The former is a contradiction of two absolutely incompatible principles whose irreconcilable differences result in a third term composed of neither one nor the other, but both. Kant refers to this situation as "nonsense," much like a body "at one and the same time in motion and not in motion." "Real" opposition, however, is based on a form of cancellation: "a motory force of a body in one direction and an equal force of the same body in an opposite direction is not incompatible"; the result is the creation of a third term, "namely rest," which is not only "real and representable" but produced by the neutralization of the conflicting terms.[21] The contradiction in "real" opposition, therefore, produces "inaction": "two equal forces acting in opposite directions, both being finite and each distinguished from the other by its direction only, must neutralize or reduce each other to inaction" (1:299). A body at rest is such inaction. In "logical" contradiction, however, the opposition of the two forces does not cancel them; they exist as a third term much like a Moebius strip of simultaneous and conflicting categories. It is this third term, characterized not by erasure but by an irreconcilable contradiction of differences, that Coleridge claims to be the basis of transcendental philosophy, for such philosophy demands that "these forces should be assumed to be both alike infinite, both alike indestructible." The products of these "two inherent indestructible yet counteracting forces" will be "results or generations to which their interpenetration gives existence, in the living principle and in the process of our own self-consciousness" (1:299). In a later passage, Coleridge identifies this third term as "tertium aliquid" or "finite generation." He does not elucidate further on the precise nature of the "tertium aliquid," aside from noting that it "can be no other than an inter-penetration of the counteracting powers, partaking of both" (1:300).

Carlyle's familiarity with Coleridge has been documented by Charles Richard Sanders, who describes Carlyle's attitude to the Sage at Highgate as essentially an ambivalent one; uneasy with Coleridge's personality, Carlyle nevertheless respects the man for his genius and cares sufficiently to justify Coleridge's obscurity to the public. In an article on Novalis, published in *Foreign Review*, Carlyle, "after declaring Coleridge to be neither so unintelligible nor so profound as Novalis," says that "the English reading public did not do justice to Coleridge's books such as *The Friend* and the *Biographia Literaria*."[22] In *Carlyle and German Thought*, Charles Frederick Harrold claims that Coleridge is "one of many quasi-anonymous but fertilizing agencies in Carlyle's intellectual development between 1816 and 1830."[23] Rosemary Ashton similarly notes that "Coleridge's writings and reputation helped to shape Carlyle's response to German philosophy."[24] Carlyle's interest in transcendentalism is so intense that he would have been familiar with the infamous chapter 13. He would probably have been quite receptive to Coleridge's "tertium aliquid," for he would have seen in this third term of irreconcilable differences the power of the motivated sign. In this third term which seeks not to reconcile differences through formulas, Carlyle would have seen the agencies of a prophetic Imaginary. Indeed, his "Chaos of Being" sounds temptingly like a derivative of Coleridge's "tertium aliquid": "it is an ever-living, ever-working Chaos of Being, wherein shape after shape bodies itself forth from innumerable elements" (W, 27:88).

Despite his confident assurance to readers that *The Critique of Pure Reason* is "by no means the hardest task they have tried" (W, 26:75), Carlyle's knowledge of Kant is, according to Harrold and Ashton, limited[25]. Ashton claims that Carlyle has not read enough of the *Critique* to have grasped the significance of *Vernunft* or *Verstand* and that his explanation of the two terms in "State of German Literature" is unconsciously much closer to Coleridge than to Kant.[26] Defining the two terms as he understands Kant to mean them, Carlyle writes: "Reason discerns Truth itself, the absolutely and primitively *True*;

while Understanding discerns only *relations*, and cannot decide without *if*" (W, 26:82). Whether or not Carlyle does fully understand Kant's terms is immaterial here; what this passage demonstrates is that Carlyle is familiar enough with Kant to have recognized the conditionality implicit in *Verstand* and the unconditional nature of *Vernunft*. Fritz Martin, in his introduction to Schelling's early writings, claims that the form of *Verstand* is "always *if then*. They [sic] are always *conditional*." Such conditionality is reflected, as well, in the etymology of the word *Verstand*: "In a market place, a tradesman sets up his *Stand*, a table with two end posts supporting a canvas top like a pup tent. It announces: Here I am, taking my *stand* for doing business." The market associations in the root "stand" of *Verstand* emphasize its conditional nature; supported by something firm, fixed, public, *Verstand* points not to itself for value, but to an exchange imperative. It is transitive because it is not a self-sufficient term; it points to a category outside itself for validation. It is, in effect, a means to an end. By contrast, *Vernunft* is an end in itself. The root of *Vernunft* is "nehmen" or "to take, to get hold of": "*Wir nehmen es* means we take it. *Wir nehmen an*, 'we take it that' or we *a*ccept, or else we *a*ssume (from Latin *ad-sumere*)."[27] Implicit in the word "assume" is the notion of unconditionality. We assume because we do not have before us a body of knowledge summed up and accounted for in objective terms; we assume because we are willing to accept what has not been previously established. From Kant, Carlyle garners not only the metaphysical and aesthetic outline of transcendentalism but the idea that intuition, *Vernunft*, constitutes the basis of an intransitive[28] and motivated third term.

Much of what Carlyle claims for *Verstand* and *Vernunft* can be gleaned from Kant's preface to the second edition of *The Critique of Pure Reason*, published in 1787. Ashton states that Carlyle has not read beyond the first hundred and fifty pages of Kant's *Critique*;[29] he does not have to, because the distinction he advances between Reason and Understanding is the distinction Kant proffers in the second preface. Kant's thesis as stated in the second preface is that the unconditioned is a necessary condition of the conditional: "For what necessarily forces us to transcend the limits of experience and of all appearances is the *unconditioned*, which reason [*Vernunft*] by necessity and by right, demands in things in themselves, as required to complete the series of conditions."[30] *Vernunft's* acceptance of unconditionality releases it from the categories of abstraction, that is, from the necessity of transitive validation by something outside itself. This Kant makes clear in his second preface to *The Critique of Pure Reason*, where he criticizes the state of "theoretical logic" as a "closed and completed body of doctrine" because "its sole concern is to give an exhaustive exposition and strict proof of formal rules of all thought" (17). Such logic, Kant states, is "propaedeutic"; it points towards a higher system of knowledge for validation; as such, it is superficial, constituting "only the vestibule of the sciences." Logic which relates to the object as "merely determining it and its concept" is therefore insufficient. What Kant sees as a necessary complement to this form of "theoretical reason" is "pure reason" or *Vernunft*, that part "in which reason determines its object completely *a priori*." *Vernunft* has to be dealt with separately in order that it not be confounded with "other sources." Here Kant compares the logic of theoretical abstraction to a runaway economy: "For it is bad management if we blindly pay out what comes in, and are not able when the income falls into arrears, to distinguish what part of it can justify expenditure and in which line we must make reductions" (18). The state of philosophy, according to Kant, is in need of "fiscal" restructuring. A purely theoretical abstraction of the subject is comparable to blind expenditure, to an expenditure based on the logic of general equivalence; that is, we pay blindly what comes in because we equate all purchases under a general comprehensive term without taking the steps to distinguish between a genuine justification of expense and "counterfeit" wares. An unconditional subject made necessarily part of the conditional by *Vernunft* becomes, for Kant, a judicious economy of metaphysics, for here the logic of general equivalence is supplanted by the motivated economy of *Vernunft*, under which assumptions are not rejected as improbable but motivated and expressed by the necessary.

What Kant calls his "Copernican Revolution" in metaphysics is his extension of experience into the unconditional realm. Logic, he claims, has not been able to determine the existence of things "a priori," that is "by means of concepts," because it is trapped within a conditional notion of knowledge as knowledge of things-in-themselves. We ask intuition in this case to "conform to the constitution of the objects"; but if we ask the "object (as object of the senses) [to conform] to the constitution of our faculty of intuition" (22) – that is, if we release knowledge from its conditional nature to apprehend an unconditional accommodation of things, not as they are in themselves, but as they *seem* – then a metaphysical science determining "a priori" the existence of things is possible: "If, then, on the supposition that our empirical knowledge conforms to objects as things in themselves, we find that the unconditioned *cannot be thought without contradiction*, and that when, on the other hand, we suppose that our representation of things, as they are given to us, does not conform to these things as they are in themselves, but these objects, as appearances, conform to our mode of representation, *the contradiction vanishes*" (24). Transcendental philosophy is worth the expense of intellectual engagement because it does not close doors to "irreconcilable differences." Instead of rejecting things outside us as non-existent, *Vernunft* is able to negotiate these things into a "logical opposition" – they are both appearances and actual entities (28). In other words, Kant's transcendental synthesis seeks not to abstract from experience, but to receive the "manifold" (many in one) of the material before it. Transcendental synthesis is the "act of putting different representations together and of grasping what is manifold in them in one [act of] knowledge." It seeks not to reduce the manifold to one term but to gather the manifold in one *act* of knowledge, that is, to create a third term which is distinctive for its multiplicity. Kant's "synthesis" is the "logical" opposition Coleridge refers to in *Biographia Literaria*; its third term is not a reconciliation of opposites, but a "crude and confused" mass, as indeed all incompatible contradictions are, and may "therefore [be] in need of analysis" (111) The very intransitive nature of Kant's *Vernunft* rests on its assumption of unconditionality or its prerogative as a synecdoche of the whole.[31]

It is not surprising that Kant uses an economic analogy to launch his discussion of *Vernunft*. He was an ardent reader of Adam Smith,[32] whose *Enquiry into the Wealth of Nations* provides a correlative to Kant's discussion of motivated reason. In many ways, Kant echoes Smith's injunction that a judicious regulation of paper currency is essential if one is not to contract debts. According to Smith, financial collapse proceeds from an unjustified faith in the logic of general equivalence or paper credit. His account of the injudicious method of "drawing," a form of borrowing from the bank on the basis of "unanchored" promissory notes, points to its drawback as a method of fiscal return based entirely on "fictitious" payment (*Wealth*, 1:331). For Smith, paper currency is viable only if it is "anchored" to some extent in real and solid gold reserves; in fact, his "economic" sanction of paper currency rests precisely on its dual nature as part substance (gold) and part trope (substitute for gold). By making the circulation of promissory notes dependent on a smaller reserve of gold and silver, a banker is able to free the remaining portion of the reserve for foreign trade; at the same time, he is able to negotiate an exchange at home which transcends the contradiction inherent in the paper notes (these promissory notes are part and yet not part of the gold and silver reserves). Smith states that these notes cannot be used for foreign commerce because they are not recognized by foreign nations as "real" money; their "legitimacy" at home, however, allows the remaining "real" reserve to be mobilized for foreign trade (1:311). It is the "motivated" nature of these notes which allows the bankers to negotiate, as it were, with one foot on substance, the other on trope, an exchange that is possible only because the contradictions within the paper notes are not erased or cancelled out, but made to exist within the logistics of the currency itself: the paper notes are viable because they are neither one nor the other, but synecdoches of the whole. Should these paper notes be entirely free from existent gold and silver reserves, their circulation could result in inflationary collapse; should they be entirely dependent on the reserves, bankers would not be able to free portions of the reserve for further profit in foreign trading. The motivated relationship between the notes and the reserves allows the notes to bring about a well-justified exchange. In effect, the currency of these notes depends on the public's willingness to motivate the arbitrary by making a transcendental leap of faith, and their willingness to do so is anchored in their belief that the banker who is issuing these notes is enabled by his reserves to make payment upon demand (1:310).

While Smith seems quite enthusiastic about the judicious use of paper currency, he is also adamant that one should place one's feet firmly on the ground in matters of financial speculation. Declaiming against the injudicious use of promissory currency by what he calls "prodigal projectors," Smith spends almost an entire chapter on the risks which over-trading in paper currency can incur (1:302–50). What we have in the judicious use of paper currency, however, is not "fictitious" payment or exchange, that is, empty promises based on depleted reserves, but a material transaction with gold-supported currency. Smith's insistent demand that profit be made material, that is, reverted to use value, appears in a later passage when he makes clear that the "new fund" generated through the circulation of paper currency should be used only for the purchase of additional stock in order to "maintain and employ an additional number of industrious people, who re-produce, with a profit, the value of their annual consumption" (1:312). The exchange, therefore, effects not more money, but labour; not an abstracted measure of general equivalence, but further engagement and satisfaction of bodily needs: "though the wages of the workmen are commonly paid to him in money, his real revenue ... consists, not in money, but in the money's worth; not in the metal pieces, but in what can be got for them" (1:313).

This anchoring of profit and return on labour, not money, can be seen as well in Kant's discussion of the categorical imperative. According to Susan Shell, both Kant and Smith understand that "universal human need establishes a natural market whereby objects of desire are priced according to the cost of the human labour which produced them." One consequence of this subjection of labour to market demand is the "reduction of men to the status of commodities, interchangeable with other instruments and deriving their value from the contingencies of human desire." Kant's solution lies in morality – the "only condition under which a rational human being can be an end in himself";[33] it is the only condition under which an object ceases to be a means or a market price. This condition, under which "man *exists* as an end in himself, *not merely as a means* to be arbitrarily used by this or that will,"[34] is the supreme expression of the categorical imperative – the unconditional value in human morality.[35]

Kant, like Smith, is aware that this unconditional expression of value in morality is an idea to which few would unconditionally subscribe; the "kingdom of ends" remains "only an ideal."[36] In the practical affairs of men, human good is effected not so much by the categorical imperative as by the circulation of its trope. Kant explains this psychology of human deception in a manner similar to Smith's explanation of the profitable returns engendered by a "counterfeit" currency:

Every human virtue in circulation is small change; only a child takes it for real gold. Nevertheless, it is better to circulate pocket pieces than nothing at all. In the end, they can be converted into genuine gold coin, though at a considerable discount. To pass them off as nothing but counters which have no value, to say with the sarcastic Swift that "Honesty [is] a pair of Shoes worn out in the Dirt" ... for the sake of preventing anyone from believing in virtue, all this is high treason perpetrated upon humanity. Even the appearance of the good in others must have value for us, because in the long run something serious can come from such a play with pretenses which gain respect even if they do not deserve to.[37]

Despite its "counterfeit" position as a trope, human virtue, like the counters and tokens of circulating currency, can indeed generate good, for it is better to circulate "pocket pieces" than "nothing at all." Eventually, these pocket pieces of "arbitrary" signs might become motivated enough to be converted into "genuine gold coin." It is only when the trope is taken for substance, that is when we cease to see the good in us as an "illusion," that we seriously run the risk of being deceived. "In general," writes Kant, "everything that we call decency (decorum) is ... just a beautiful illusion."[38] Human virtue is, in general, a means to an end, a "counter" of transitive value. However, for those willing to make the transition to the intransitive "kingdom of ends," this counterfeit currency can be motivated, that is, converted to real gold. Our moral security is jeopardized only when we take the counters for real gold, the trope for substance.

Sound fiscal policy in the Kantian scheme of things is one which suspends the abstract within the material, the trope within substance, the motivated within the arbitrary, much like the Carlylean "symbol" which "bodies forth" the infinite in the finite. This dual imperative of the symbol is a concept which Carlyle would have encountered not only in Coleridge's discussion of the "tertium aliquid" but also in his distinction between symbol and allegory. For Coleridge, an allegory is an abstraction of an abstraction; it is produced by a "counterfeit product of the mechanical understanding," a "principal" which is even more worthless than its "phantom proxy."[39] Coleridge's allegory is a transitive and arbitrary term whose validity resides not in itself but in another or higher term. Like "a string of blind men, each holding the skirt of the man before him, reaching far out of sight, but all moving without the least deviation in one strait line," the allegory is "infinite blindness" (*Biographia Literaria*, 1:266). The symbol, by contrast, is a motivated sign. It "partakes of the reality which it renders intelligible"; "it enunciates the whole" and "abides itself as a living part in that unity of which it is the representative" (*Works*, 1:437–8), and by doing so, it is "one which is its own predicate" (*Biographia Literaria*, 1:268). Coleridge's symbol is an extension of Kant's *Vernunft*, for the basis of motivation in both is synecdoche, the part for the whole. In *Aids to Reflection*, he describes the symbol as a "sign included in the idea which it represents": "an actual part chosen to represent the whole as a lip with a chin prominent is a symbol of man" (*Works*, 1:270). Coleridge, a Greek scholar, would have been aware of the original synecdochic dimension of the Greek "symbolon." As John A. Hodgson states in *Coleridge, Shelley and Transcendental Inquiry*, "Coleridge, with his great interest in etymology, his excellent Greek, and his precocious immersion in the Neoplatonic tradition ... would have known and appreciated this" – the idea that "a *symbolon* was a particular token of recognition – half of a whole object, such as a die, coin, or ring, which could later be joined to the other half as proof of identity or purpose."[40] As a particular form of synecdochic imagination, Coleridge's symbol is intransitive; it does not point to an external agency for equivalence. This he makes clear in two passages in *Aids to Reflection*.

The first passage is a commentary on aphorism VII in the section entitled "Aphorisms on that which is Indeed Spiritual Religion." This passage includes, first of all, Coleridge's distinction between analogy and metaphor and, by extension, symbol and allegory. The metaphor, Coleridge claims, is allegorical. It "expresse[s] a different subject but with a resemblance"; it establishes an "equivalence" between two unlike entities; it is, "in its own nature," "a transcendent act," but falls short of being so because it equates a transcendent effect with an ordinary or more acceptable cause: a metaphor "produces sundry effects, each of which is the same kind with an effect produced by a cause well known and of ordinary occurrence." The designation of these effects "by a succession of names borrowed from their ordinary causes" is metaphorical language (*Works*, 1:235). In a later commentary on this passage, Coleridge defines the metaphor as a movement towards general equivalence: "the purpose of a metaphor is to illustrate a something less known by a partial identification of it with some other thing better understood, or at least more familiar" (*Works*, 1:308). Thus the Pauline metaphors of Redemption, which Coleridge identifies as expiation, reconciliation, ransom, and debt, remain untenable, since they serve to reduce the unutterable miracle and mystery of the Redemption to terms "equally familiar to all, and yet having a special interest for the Jewish converts" (*Works*, 1:309) – the language of debt and repayment. In typically Coleridgean fashion, he unfolds in his footnote the etymology of the Greek derivatives of these terms. Reconciliation, he notes, is used in Greek as a term for "a money-changer, or one who takes the debased currency ... in exchange for sterling coin or bullion"; in older Greek writers, the verb "to reconcile" means "to exchange for an opposite," as in the phrase "He exchanged within himself enmity for friendship (that is, he reconciled himself) with his party," or, in more current terms, he "made it up with them" or "he made up the difference." Coleridge suggests that this sense of reconciliation (the making up of the difference) is equivalent to the Hebrew word for "atonement," which "has its radical [in the sense of root] or visual image in *copher*, pitch." To "pitch" is "to unite," the word expressing both "the act ... [of] bringing together what had been previously separated, and the means, or material by which the re-union is effected as in [the] English verbs, to caulk, to solder, to *poy* or pay (from *poix* pitch)." Coleridge finally associates the word "reconciliation" with ransom by citing its use in the Epistle to Timothy as an "equivalent term" (*Works*, 1:309). It is this transitive nature of the metaphor, its convenient "synonimization" with equivalent terms, its reduction to arbitrary and current figures of speech that Coleridge singles out to be problematic in metaphors.

In his bracketed mathematical declension of the transcendent X, Coleridge parodies the reductionism that the "equating" factor in similitudes and metaphors imposes on language: "Now let X signify a transcendent, that is, a cause beyond our comprehension, and not within the sphere of sensible experience; and, on the other hand, let A, B, C and D represent each one known and familiar cause, in reference to some single and characteristic effect: namely A in reference to k, B to l, C to m and D to n. Then I say X + k l m n is in different places expressed by A + k; B + l; C + m; D + n. And these I should call metaphorical exponents of X" (*Works*, 1:310). In this somewhat tongue-in-cheek exponential reduction of the metaphor, Coleridge produces the simplification of the transcendent term (a cause beyond our comprehension) into mathematical equations of value. If the purpose of such exponential reduction is to make the transcendent X comprehensible to all, then the metaphor in Coleridge's view is as much an agency of limitation as it is of intelligibility. Its transitive nature is illustrated in the reductionism the Pauline metaphors of debt and ransom impose on the incomprehensible mystery of Redemption. The metaphor is a form of synonimization; its attempt to reconcile differences through equivalence makes it an extension of "common-sense."

In a footnote in chapter 4 of the *Biographia Literaria*, Coleridge associates common-sense language with this "reconciliatory" imperative: men of common sense naturalize distinctions between words; they remove "equivocation" either by "the substitution of a new word, or by the appropriation of one of the two or more words that had before been used promiscuously." They create a language of "such general currency" that it thinks for them "like the sliding rule which is the mechanic's safe substitute for arithmetical knowledge" (1:86). Allegorical language, in its equation of cause with effect, is for Coleridge a variant of common sense. It is as intelligible, therefore, as a merchant's account book. This intelligibility Coleridge elaborates in an anecdote in *Aids to Reflection*:

A sum of £1000 is due from James to Peter, for which James has given a bond. He is insolvent and the bond is on the point of being put in suit against him, to James' utter ruin. At this moment, Matthew steps in, pays Peter the thousand pounds, and discharges the bond. In this case, no man would hesitate to admit, that a complete satisfaction had been made to Peter. Matthew's £1000 is a perfect equivalence for the sum which James was bound to have paid and which Peter had lent. It is the same thing, and this is altogether a question of things. (*Works*, 1:314)

The question of metaphor is not only a question of things; it is a question of the mechanics of a money economy. The equivalence understood in Matthew's payment of debt is unequivocally clear and straightforward. A thousand pounds is a thousand pounds, and, in the allegorical scheme of similitudes, the two sums are made to be "the same thing"; like the opposed categories in a "real opposition," which neutralize each other into a perfect equilibrium, the metaphor resolves differences into an easy resemblance. It is this easy resemblance which Coleridge claims to be impossible in the symbol:

> Now instead of James's being indebted to Peter in a sum of money which (he having become insolvent) Matthew pays for him, let me put the case, that James had been guilty of the basest and most hard-hearted ingratitude to a most worthy and affectionate mother ... who ... had sacrificed her health and the far greater part of her resources to rescue him from ... his follies and excesses ... and to procure for him the means of his present rank and affluence – all which he had repaid by neglect, desertion, and open profligacy. Here the mother stands in the relation of the creditor: and here too, I will suppose the same generous friend to interfere, and to perform with the greatest ... constancy all those duties of a grateful and affectionate son, which James ought to have performed. Will this satisfy the mother's claim on James ...? (*Works*, 1:314–15)

By no means, claims Coleridge, for Matthew's assumption of James's gratitude can only aggravate the mother's misery. Should Matthew declare to the mother that his actions on James's behalf would satisfy the "debt," the mother would have the right to protest his words as insult. Matthew's assumption of James's "debt" cannot be as easily resolved in this situation, for Matthew's "generosity" can only intensify the mother's sense of abandonment: "Must not the contrast of [James's] merits magnify his demerits in his mother's eye ...?" (*Works*, 1:315). However, should James, by the force of Matthew's example, be moved to become a dutiful son, the mother would indeed have reason to be wholly satisfied. In both cases, then, the effect on James would be similar; James the debtor and James the undutiful son have both been "liberated from a grievous burthen." In both cases, the liberation is due to the "act and free grace of another." The only difference is that the effect in the former case requires no "reaction or co-agency" on the part of James, while in the latter case the "reconciliation" cannot be effected without the voluntary and "inward co-agency" (*Works*, 1:315) of James's repentance.

It is this "inward co-agency" which Coleridge suggests is the basis of the symbol. The "tautegorical" nature of the symbol, by which the same subject is expressed, but with a "difference," demands that the gestures of reconciliation become the very "body" of repentance. Thus, the symbol generates a "logical opposition," by which two opposed forces produce, not equilibrium, but a third term of irreconcilable differences. The symbol comprehends the motivated dynamics of a barter economy such that the gestures of reconciliation on Matthew's part cannot suffice as arbitrary signs; only through their motivation by a genuine repentance on James's part can James's gestures be taken as symbolic; only when these gestures become the material or bodily expression of an inward repentance can they be seen as symbolic. For Coleridge, the doctrine of redemption from sin is more than a mere settling of debts; it supplies the Christian with "motives and reasons for the divinity of the Redeemer" that are "coercive subjectively," that is, "in the economy of his [the Christian's] own soul" (*Works*, 1:222). If the metaphor is a question of things, the symbol is a question of spirit within things; the spirit which has "no other predicate than its own self" (*Biographia Literaria*, 1:278n3) is symbolized by the coincidence of spirit and wheel in Ezekiel's Wheel. The economy of turn and return implicit in the wheel is the crux of its redemptive power.

Coleridge's objection to Wordsworth's language of "real men" is an objection to its removal from such redemptive economy. In chapter 22 of *Biographia Literaria*, he distinguishes between words used in "real life" as the "*arbitrary marks* of thought, our smooth market-coin of intercourse with the image and superscription worn out by currency," and the motivated language of art, used to "body forth the inward state of a person speaking" (2:122). This concern with a motivated language emerges as well in the curious relationship between chapters 12 and 13 of *Biographia Literaria*.

Chapter 12 is dominated by the bias of intelligibility; its reliance on theorems is indicative of the imperialism of "theoria" (seeing). Chapter 13, by contrast, is the material and opaque which is rendered through the symbol – the symbol of the Gothic church. Describing the effect produced on him by Coleridge's chapter on the imagination, the unknown correspondent expresses his "feelings" in Gothic terms: "The effect of my feelings ... I cannot better represent than by supposing myself to have known only our light airy modern chapels of ease, and then for the first time to have been placed, and left alone, in one of our largest Gothic cathedrals in a gusty moonlight night of autumn. 'Now in glimmer, and now in gloom'; often in palpable darkness and not without a chilly sensation of terror ... In short, what I had supposed substances were thinned away into shadows, while every where shadows were deepened into substances" (1:301). The Gothic cathedral as symbol stands as a point of chiastic exchange (shadows become substances and substances shadows); it is an exchange fraught with the barter dimensions of a Lacanian

Imaginary. The Gothic cathedral as symbol is precisely what the correspondent as "other" becomes in Coleridge's text: the circle which turns from the straight road of "theoria" towards an "ulterior consciousness" not dependent on sight, a consciousness Coleridge refers to as a "land of darkness, a perfect *Anti-Goshen*" (1:243). Moreover, the correspondent urges Coleridge to withhold publication of his treatise on the Imagination because the public is not ready for it: "you have been obliged to omit so many links, from the necessity of compression, that what remains, looks ... like the fragments of the winding steps of an old ruined tower" (1:302–3).

Coleridge's Gothic tower stands as the material expression of its specular other. Carlyle's Gothicism in *The French Revolution* stands as the material expression of the Coleridgean symbol. In *Sartor Resartus*, he defines the symbol as "concealment ... yet revelation," Silence and Speech "acting together" into a "double significance" (W, 1:175). In *The French Revolution*, he associates the symbol with kingship – "a Symbol of true Guidance in return for loving Obedience" (W, 2:9), a reciprocity comprehended in the ideal coincidence of sovereign and state. If mechanism turns man into a utilitarian allegory by making him fancy himself a "dead Iron-Balance for weighing Pains and Pleasures," calculating equivalence from "one huge Manger, filled with hay and thistles to be weighed against each other" (W, 1:176), then only the dynamic can produce the symbol. As union of extrinsic and intrinsic value, the symbol stands as a manifestation of the "Godlike" to "Sense" (W, 1:178); its infinite character is revealed in the intransitive nature of its sign, that is, in its demand that its significance be "anew inquired into, and anew made manifest" (W, 1:179). Unlike the allegory, whose signified holds a tyrannical power over the signifier, the symbol, as motivated sign, must accept the loss of power as a condition of its motivation. In short, the symbol must accept the unconditionality of Kant's *Vernunft* to be intrinsic to its being; by its very nature, the symbol is an embodying as much as a disembodying, a shaping of new matter as much as a dispersal of matter, what Foucault, in "The Order of Discourse," characterizes as the "event": "the event is not of the order of bodies. And yet it is not something immaterial either; it is always at the level of materiality that it takes effect, that it is effect; it has its locus and it consists in the relation, the coexistence, and dispersion, the overlapping, the accumulation, and the selection of material elements ... the philosophy of the event should move in the ... paradoxical direction of a materialism of the incorporeal."[41] If allegory is the exercise of a discourse of power, the symbol, by its character as "event," is a dispersion of power. Carlyle's symbol is both a crowning and an uncrowning of the signifier for his symbol questions the basis of "sovereignty": does the sovereign reside in what is extrinsically established by convention? or does it reside in an intrinsic coincidence of sign and meaning? In other words, does the "power" of the signifier reside in its dynamics as "event"?

If Carlyle's Gothicism stands as a material expression of this "event," it also does so as a deliberate response to Burke's extrinsic signifier in his *Reflections on the Revolution in France*. Burke's letter stands as a treatise on substance, for Burke sees the sovereign as a necessary signifier, a "god-term" made substance by convention. Thus the Crown is invested with the power of wealth, which Burke aligns with the flourishing commercial sense of a Whig government. In his comparison of the French "assignats" to British paper currency, Burke locates the difference in the disjunction between sign and substance: "In fact it might easily be shewn, that our paper wealth, instead of lessening the real coin, has a tendency to increase it; instead of being a substitute for money, it only facilitates its entry, its exit and its circulation; that it is the symbol of prosperity, and not the badge of distress. Never was a scarcity of cash, and an exuberance of paper, a subject of complaint in this nation" (250).[42] English paper currency is a sign of a flourishing economy because it is based solidly on gold reserves; it has its "origin in cash actually deposited" and is therefore "convertible, at pleasure, in an instant, and without the smallest loss, into cash again" (249). The English signifier is therefore solidly entrenched in substance; French paper currency, by contrast, is purely "fictitious representation" (249); its issuance is not based on solid fiscal reserves, as can be seen in the readiness with which French "assignats" were "fitted out" as remedies to the National Debt (251). The paper currency of the French is as empty a signifier as the coffers of these "philosophic financiers" (251) whose solution to the fiscal crisis of France is as prodigal as the revolutionaries' attempt at "cashiering the King." For Burke, the problem of the Revolution is essentially an economic one; the disjunction of sign from substance, crown from sovereign power, has unleashed "a species of political monster, which has always ended by devouring those who have produced it" (228–9). This monster Burke identifies as a *"military democracy"* (228), a tyrannical consolidation of the arbitrary signifier into allegory. The "monied interests" of an emergent bourgeoisie, confiscating the property of landed aristocracy, have squandered the wealth of nations in an unprecedented abuse of the tropological value of the sign.

In his analysis, Burke locates the source of fiscal mismanagement in the revolutionaries' appropriation of sign over substance. They sold the confiscated Church property not for solid cash, but for "fictitious" payment; by the "late resolutions of the national assembly," these lands were delivered to the "highest bidder," who was not required to make full payment in cash, but only to submit a "downpayment": "*a certain portion only of the purchase money [was] to be laid down*" and a "period of twelve years [was] to be given for the payment of the rest." The result was that the transaction became a form of fictional payment, for the project "let in a body of purchasers without money." Burke speculates on the abuse which could result from this "philosophic" purchase: the purchasers, to satisfy the "mortgage" from the rents as they accrue, would be in an apt position to "wring" all they could "from the miserable peasant" (137). Another example of such "philosophic" finance emerges in Burke's criticism of the French issuance of paper currency to satisfy the old debt: "instead of paying the old debt, [the revolutionaries] contracted a new debt, at 3 per cent creating a new paper currency, founded on an eventual sale of church lands." In a passage which reminds us of the prodigal speculators of Smith's *Wealth of Nations*, Burke depicts this paper currency as a fiction based on fiction: "[the revolutionaries] issued this paper currency to satisfy in the first instance chiefly the demands made upon them by the *Bank of discount*, the great machine, or paper-mill, of their fictitious wealth" (135). Burke associates French paper currency with a "philosophic" system which has no base in substance. English currency he grounds in the substance of contractarian ideology – "the great primaeval contract of eternal society ... according to a fixed compact sanctioned by the inviolable oath which holds all physical and all moral natures, each in their appointed place" (110). Substance, for Burke, is the harnessing of energies within the restraints of convention; these energies, he claims, have "always existed in nature." Some are "unserviceable, some noxious, some no better than a sport to children."

But these energies are useless unless a "contemplative ability, combining with practic skill, [tames] their wild nature, [subdues] them to use and [renders] them at once the most powerful and the most intractable agents, in subservience to the great views and designs of men" (173–4). This "contemplative ability" resides not in the arbitrary will, but in the established and "publick consolation" (112) of convention: "I cannot conceive," Burke writes, "how any man can have brought himself to that pitch of presumption, to consider his country as nothing but *carte blanche*, upon which he may scribble whatever he pleases" (172). Substance, for Burke, resides in "the accumulation of vast libraries," in the "great collections of antient records, medals and coins, which attest and explain laws and customs," in "paintings and statues," and in the "grand monuments of the dead, which continue the regards and connexions of life beyond the grave" (177). Substance as inscription, as the permanent and indelible "stamp of our forefathers" (99), cannot accommodate the rupture of the sign; is it necessary therefore, he asks, that the "whole fabric should be at once pulled down and the area cleared for the erection of a theoretic, experimental edifice in its place?" (141)

Carlyle's answer in *The French Revolution* is that substance cannot be confounded with sign, that the "revolutionary" debt is a necessary rupture of the sign and that the implications of this debt can be only *partially* understood within a political allegory of fiscal mismanagement. Burke's accounting of the Revolution in economic terms remains only an allegorical accommodation of the event. If the Revolution is to become more than a decapitated signifier, it has to be a revolution which "lies in the heart and mind of every violent-speaking, of every violent-thinking Frenchman" (*W*, 2:214). Burke sees the Revolution as a Faustian sale, the "brave people" having sacrificed all for an equivocal liberty (*Reflections*, 149). The "'all-atoning name' of Liberty" cannot settle the debt, for it can only answer in the most equivalent terms, much like bidding at an auction, and when "leaders choose to make themselves bidders at an auction of popularity, their talents, in the construction of the state, will be of no service" (263). Thus, they become "flatterers" instead of "legislators" and he will be elected who can produce the most "splendidly popular" scheme (264). In their bid for liberty, the French have sold their inheritance (substance) for an arbitrary signifier – the current coin of popular election. For Burke, the French Revolution's turning into a "shop of horrors" (94) is an allegory of economic collapse.

If the allegory comprehends an arbitrary and tyrannical system of signification, much like the "money economy of the law of the Father," its solution is as futile as the Burkean dream of substance for, according to Carlyle, "ours is a most fictile world ... A world not fixable; not fathomable" (*W*, 2:6). We cannot immure ourselves within a prison-house of substance any more than within "Phantasms" and "Paper models" (*W*, 4:322). Our only recourse is to the Carlylean symbol, which, in its return to the "barter economy" of a repressed Imaginary, transmutes a superannuated sign into a necessary and motivated "event." Burke's analysis rejects the "shop of horrors" as a "botched-up" sale, but Carlyle sees in the economics of terror the economy of the event. If, as Foucault suggests, discourse is a "violence we do to things,"[43] every articulation carries within it the potential for an economics of terror; but if we perceive this violence as a necessarily synecdochic materialism of the immaterial, then the economics of terror can be transmuted into a holistic economy of disruption and solution: "Consider it well, the Event, the thing which can be spoken of and recorded, is it not, in all cases, some disruption, some solution of continuity?" (W, 2:27). What remains to be seen in Carlyle's *French Revolution* is his explicit deployment of the economics of terror within Gothic discourse. Within this context, Carlyle's interest in Goethe's *Faust* is not surprising, for he saw in Goethe's Gothicism a corollary to an abortive Faustian exchange.

2 Faustian Analogues

Despite its initially unfavourable reception in Britain,[1] Goethe's *Faust* remains an influential work. It is no coincidence that subsequent to the publication of part 1 of *Faust*, we find in England a series of "Faustian texts," all predicated on the logistics of the wager. The Faustian wager becomes the pivotal argument in two highly popular Gothic works: Lewis's *The Monk* and Maturin's *Melmoth the Wanderer*. Here the wager participates as idiom of a commercial bargain – one sells one's soul in exchange for the devil's word, but, in a classic "sleight-of-hand," the wages of sin become the marks of deficit when the word, made current by an inflationary economy, plunges its reader into a "recessionary" text. It is this rupture in the "economics" of the word that carries the mark of Satan, and the Gothicism of Lewis and Maturin resides precisely in their use of terror as strategy of exposure. The text becomes a source of betrayal when what at first appears a profitable bargain is unmasked as a "botched-up" sale; in this sense, reading emerges as an abortive wager. If the Gothic temper is that of an unrelenting ironist, then the "Gothicism" of Lewis and Maturin rests on their insistence that neither language nor system is immune to betrayal. Terror, in this context, is the return of the repressed. In *Melmoth the Wanderer*, for example, John Melmoth reads an old manuscript in his uncle's room, a manuscript he assumes to contain the key to the perverse behaviour of his uncle. The reading, however, initiates a series of exchanges (narratives) which, instead of fulfilling the "contractual" terms a reader expects from a text ensuring comprehensibility and transmission of ideas, opens into other alien and unresolved texts. In Lewis's monk, Ambrosio, we find a similar betrayal by the allegorical word. Ambrosio's sexual repression leads to his iniquitous association with Matilda. His lust for Matilda becomes yet another sign of a depleted and bankrupt monastic system; the terror of the text is unleashed when Ambrosio "sells" himself body and soul to the fiend and finds the sale a superannuated allegory. The mark of Satan in Gothic discourse is the word's betrayal of the reader. What I intend to pursue in this chapter are the Faustian analogues that provided Carlyle with an economic metaphor of reading. I will trace the motif of the betrayal as it is deployed in *Faust* and subsequent Gothic romances in order to situate its position within "The Diamond Necklace," an experimental narrative that points the way towards revisionary Gothicism in *The French Revolution*.

In *Faust*, the wager is deployed in *two* senses at *two* pivotal moments of the drama. Mephistopheles' wager with God is predicated on the former's insistence on being an unmotivated sign. Mephistopheles' claim that Faust can never be redeemed from the "downward path" (2:326)[2] is a claim for the conditional word. "If," argues Mephistopheles, "You grant me permission / to guide him gently along my road" (2:314), "You'll lose him yet" (2:312). As an unmotivated sign, Mephistopheles makes a conditional bargain with God under the most predictable terms. Mephistopheles' assumption of Faust's damnation is posited with unquestioning faith in the "currency" of satanic pacts: after all, the conventional stories of Faust provide no reprieve for one bearing the mark of Satan. This first wager is, therefore, the wager of the unmotivated sign. The second wager – that is, Faust's wager with Mephistopheles – is pledged on Faust's resistance to being such a sign (2:1692–8).

Can Faust redeem from an allegorical language the prerogatives of the symbol? This question we find to be the "business" of the Faustian wager, an exchange whose solvency depends less on the binding nature of its conditional terms than on its susceptibility to change. It is this dual sense of the wager, as a conditional bargain *and* as a possibility to transcend the conditions of the bargain, that is at the basis of the Faustian exchange. In part I, the Faustian wager is expressed under the most conditional terms:

If I should ever say to any moment:
Tarry remain! – you are so fair!
then you may lay your fetters on me,
then I will gladly be destroyed!

Yet what emerges at the end of part II is Faust's transcendence of these conditional terms. In part II, act v, Faust articulates what he has understood (perhaps unconsciously) all along that "he, only, merits freedom and existence / who wins them everyday anew" (2:11575–6). Restating the conditional terms of his wager, he invests his former words with an entirely different spirit:

> If only I might see that people's teeming life
> share their autonomy on unencumbered soil;
> then, to the moment, I could say:
> tarry a while, you are so fair –
> the traces of my days on earth
> will survive into eternity! (2:11579–84)

What was formerly a conditional statement affirming the conditional nature of the wager becomes in Faust's recapitulation a subjective statement affirming the "unconditionality" of the wagered terms: he can never see the people's teeming life or sustain the happy moment. Faust's recognition of the unconditional clause redeems him from betrayal by the word, for betrayal is a condition of the binding text, a text which aborts all avenues of change or transcendence. The "paper money" introduced by Mephistopheles to staunch the economic woes of the Emperor is a trope of such an allegorical text. The ultimate terror of being betrayed by the text, by writing, emerges not only in the volcanic "explosion" in the Great Pan masque of part II, but in Mephistopheles' recognition that the "botched up" sale is decidedly a Mephistophelean one.

The nature of this "botched-up" sale will be pursued in this chapter while we make our way through three Faustian analogues that constellate a type of "precursor" text to Carlyle's *The French Revolution*. In the Goethian categories of allegory and symbol, paper currency and redemptive value, we see the basis of an economics of terror that Carlyle comes to associate explicitly with the language and prerogatives of Gothicism. "Just as the Kantian revolution made forever impossible the return to an epistemology of certainty, *Faust* brings literature to a heightened stage of self-awareness, but this new degree of self-consciousness must be purchased at a high price, and that price is the security of unambiguous meaning."[3] It is this "purchase" that Carlyle makes when he claims in "Goethe's Helena" that what "doctrine" is stated in *Faust* is stated "emblematically and parabolically: so that it might seem as if, in Goethe's hands, the history of Faust, commencing among the realities of every-day existence, superadding to these certain spiritual agencies, and passing into a more aërial character as it proceeds, may fade away, at its termination, into a phantasmagoric region, where symbol and thing are no longer clearly distinguished; and thus the final result be curiously and significantly indicated, rather than directly exhibited" (W, 26:195). Again, in "Goethe's Works," Carlyle speaks disparagingly of the "ready-made, coloured-paper metaphors, such as can be sewed or plastered on the surface, by way of giving an ornamental finish to the rag-web" of popular literature; at the same time, he praises Goethe's figurativeness, which "lies in the very centre of his being; manifests itself as the constructing of the inward elements of a thought, as the *vital* embodiment of it" (W, 27:438). The very integrity and vitality of Goethe's symbols reside in their "phantasmagoric" quality; neither symbol nor thing, Goethe's figures remain "revelations of the mystery of all mysteries, Man's life as it actually is" (W, 27:437). Carlyle's resistance to an allegorical "accounting" of *Faust* can be seen in his rejection of the popular conflation of Euphorion with Lord Byron. Focusing on Goethe's stage remark just after Euphorion's demise – "You fancy you recognized in the dead a well-known form" – Carlyle argues for a parabolic rather than allegorical interpretation of the text: "while we fancy we recognize in the dead a well-known form, 'the bodily part instantly disappears'; and the keenest critic finds ... he can see no deeper" (W, 26:193). "Euphorion is no image of any person," Carlyle maintains, "least of all, one would think, of George Lord Byron" (W, 26:193n1).

This uneasy relationship between symbol and thing, text and reader, emerges in the economic motifs of *Faust*. The "Prelude on the Stage" opens with a direct consideration of the economics of audience appeal. The Manager states openly that his chief aim is to satisfy the demands of the public, especially the public whose taste has been formed by popular reading (2:43–5). Public appeal and a full "cash-box" become almost synonymous terms (2:54) for the Manager, whose literary sensibility is unable to transcend the mercenary motives of a hack artist. What needs the public artistic whole? he argues. They come only for entertainment that is "mindless" as "masquerade" (2:118). He proffers, therefore, a medley that is sensational and theatrical: "this is no time to stint on scenery or stage effects" (2:233–4); he likens his medley to a "strong drink" that one "gulp[s] down fast" (2:223), not for nourishment but for effect. In his drive for money, the Manager opts for a reductive and neutralizing third term: "only by mass can you subdue the masses – there's then enough for all to have their pick" (2:95–6). The Poet, by contrast, motions towards a transcendent idealism: "What glitters, lives for the moment; / What has real worth, survives for all posterity" (2:73–4).

The allegorical "glitter" of the Manager he dismisses for his own the incarnational power (2:157); it is his prerogative to endow an "unconcerned" Nature (2:142) with "life and rhythmic motion" (2:147). Yet, for all his "fine phrases" (2:216), he risks abandoning the material world for a "celestial refuge" (2:63). It is the Player, therefore, who emerges as an irreconcilable third term, accommodating both Manager and Poet within a theatrical brew "that satisfies / and yet refreshes one and all" (2:172–3). Neither a whole which subordinates the part, nor a part unable to become a whole, the Player's position wields the part as a synecdochic extension of the whole: "From the whole store of human life just grab some bit ... so that it is of interest, whatever you may pick" (2:167–9). This return to the synecdochic dimension of the fragment can be perceived as a return to the Imaginary dynamics of childhood (2:175–83).

A similar configuration issues from the relationship between Faust and Mephistopheles. The latter's insistence on being "part of the Part that first was all" (2:1349) is an insistence on a money economy of equivalence. He insists on seeing himself as a reductive term, abstracted from a dialectical whole. The economic dimension in Mephistopheles' negation emerges in Faust's description of this negation as "retail" destruction: "You can't achieve wholesale destruction / and so you've started out at retail" (2:1360–1). Mephistopheles' raillery against the intervention of light is symptomatic of a strong resistance to a dialectical third term:

> I'm part of the Part that first was all
> part of the Darkness that gave birth to Light –
> proud Light, that now contests the senior rank
> of Mother Night, disputes her rights to space;
> yet it does not succeed, however much it strives,
> because it can't escape material fetters. (2:1349–54)

Mesphistopheles' vision is Manichean; he reduces phenomenon either to pure Light or pure Night. Since he gives Night the senior rank of being the Mother that preceded Light, he is unable to accommodate the dialectical possibilities of light and darkness. In his "Theory of Colour," Goethe describes colour as "deeds of light, what it does and what it endures [suffers]."[4] A Mephistophelean universe is monochromatic because it denies the possibility of colour as "deeds of light." Goethe's belief that colour is produced by "division and opposition," "combination and union" (12:164), emerges from what he considers to be the "economy of Nature" (12:155). In his essay on "Polarity," Goethe describes Nature as having a "practical character, inclined to do much with small means where others produce little with great means" (12:155–6). To do this, "she uses the principle of life, with its inherent potential to work with the simplest phenomenon and diversify it by intensification into the most infinite and varied forms" (12:156). Division and opposition are therefore the most basic activity or "deeds" of Nature, for "[w]hatever appears in the world must divide if it is to appear to all" (12:156). For Goethe, perception is implicitly a dialectical and active experience: "In the process of what we call 'seeing,' the retina is simultaneously in different – indeed, in opposite – states. Strong but not blinding illumination works side by side with absolute darkness. At one and the same time we perceive all the intermediate degrees of light and shadow, and all the distinct qualities of colour" (12:169). While pure light "blinds" human vision, light filtered by matter produces a medium capable of being perceived. This "checkered" medium is colour as deed of light, or symbol as deed of spirit. Mephistopheles' Manichean vision refuses to see the polar conflict between light and matter as productive. "Light emanates from matter," claims Mephistopheles, "lends it beauty, / but matter checks the course of light, / and so I hope it won't be long / before they both have been annihilated" (2:1355–8).

By insisting on annihilation as the only outcome of polarity, Mephistopheles echoes the neutralizing agency of Coleridge's "real" opposition. What he fails to see is the dialectical potential within a "logical" opposition in which the third term, generated by conflict, becomes an energizing accommodation of both polar terms. This "logical" opposition, however, is the essence of the Faustian spirit. In the opening scene of part II, Faust awakens to an awareness of the fundamental economy of Nature – "to strive henceforth towards being's highest form" (2:4685). Looking at animated Nature around him, he not only hears the "myriads of living voices" (2:4687) but also perceives "colour on colour" emerging in the paradise that surrounds him (2:4692). Looking above, he perceives the sun in "full solemnity" (2:4696), but turns his gaze away "suffused with pain" (2:4703). Instead, he is "content to have the sun behind [him]" (2:4715) and looks towards the rainbow forming its "changing – unchanged arch / now clearly drawn, now evanescent" (2:4722–3), "of human striving ... a perfect symbol" (2:4725). This displacement of sun by rainbow is Faust's pursuit of the symbol, expressed as a form of barter economy. Rejecting the privileged position of an allegorical god-term, Faust chooses to articulate life as an uncertain and irreconcilable "many-hued reflection" (2:4727).

Mephistopheles' position as "allegory" is underscored in the slapstick comic tone of part 1, specifically in the "hocus pocus" of the initial conjuration scene. This farcical tone in part 1 is linked to Faust's attempt to negotiate a way out of the unmotivated sign through magic. The "hocus-pocus" produces Mephistopheles, dressed as a "wandering scholar" (2:1324), allegory of an allegorical position. The scholar as a two-dimensional and superannuated sign is delineated again in the figure of Wagner in part 1. Here, Wagner emerges as a scholar indifferent to a situation which Faust experiences as trauma – the problem of the unmotivated sign. Indeed, Faust's angst in part 1 is caused by his painful awareness of his allegorical position. His "high-vaulted, narrow" Gothic study becomes a visual emblem of a superannuated position: imprisoned by a mass of dust-covered, worm-infested volumes, he rejects scholarship as "peddling empty words" (2:385). In the first "Night" scene, he turns despairingly away from the sign of the macrocosm because he finds the sign a "mere show" (2:454). He "thirst[s] in vain" (2:459), yet finds in the sign no nourishment. He turns to the sign of the Erdgeist, which he summons before him. But the Erdgeist refuses to accommodate Faust – "Your peer is the spirit you comprehend / mine you are not" (2:512–13) – because Faust is as yet not ready for the dialectical economy of the Erdgeist. "I surge and ebb, / move to and fro! / As cradle to grave / as unending sea, / as constant change, / as life's incandescence" (2:502–7), claims the Erdgeist, while Faust stands in the study, desperately proclaiming equality with a spirit he has summoned from a book. The Erdgeist's rejection of Faust emphasizes Faust's distance from the motivated symbol. He has, as yet, only comprehended the Word as Word; only when he interprets the Word as "*Act*" (2:1237) does he unleash the diabolical and dialectical potential of his study-world. Yet Goethe is careful to emphasize that Faust's spirit of comprehension goes beyond the two-dimensionality of the Enlightenment philosophe. Wagner's "dryasdust" scholarship stands as a foil to Faust's earnestness. In Wagner, we see the characteristic ignorance of a scholar who understands language only as "rhetoric" (2:533); he beseeches Faust to give him "useful lessons" (2:527) on "declaiming" (2:522). Faust responds with the statement that language can be made persuasive only by "innate force" (2:536). Wagner's pursuit of the rhetorical properties of the word delineates his ignorance of the word as symbol, as an agency whose force comes not from "pauper baubles" made "for mankind's amusement" (2:555), but from genuine motivation. Faust himself recognizes only too well that what he has inherited from his father remains a "heap of countless, useless things" (2:658) unless motivated by use and merit (2:683). Wagner is contented with the "pleasures of the mind" that "transport us from book to book, from page to page" (2:1105); Faust is driven by two souls: "one grips the earth with all its senses; / the other struggles from the dust / to rise to high ancestral spheres" (2:1114–17). Throughout part 1, Faust is aware of the necessity of this double position. Even in the wager scene with Mephistopheles, Faust rejects the two-dimensionality of the devil's allegorical position:

> And what have you to give, poor devil!
> Has any human spirit and its aspirations
> ever been understood by such as you?
> Of course you've food that cannot satisfy,
> gold that, when held, will liquify
> quicksilver as it turns red,
> games at which none can ever win ...
> Show me the fruit that, still unplucked, will rot
> and trees that leaf each day anew!   (2:1675–87)

Allegories do not satisfy primal hunger; allegories are "fool's gold"; what Faust demands is the worth which is revealed by "unceasing activity alone" (2:1759). He is already committed to the "Act" and his wager is not so much a wager against Mephistopheles as a wager against himself – to see if he can be detoured away from a life of unceasing activity (2:1694–8). Faust's wager pits activity against distraction, and if on the surface both appear the same, they can yet be distinguished in the way that real gold can be distinguished from fool's gold, real money from paper currency. Faust's engagement of Mephistopheles is an attempt to motivate a superannuated world through magic – but this magic, like gold, must be accompanied by acute powers of discrimination. Faust's wager is that he can transcend the mere show of false magic into a genuine experience of transformation. "You are just what you are," insists Mephistopheles, "pile wigs with countless curls upon your head / wear shoes that lift you up an ell, / and still you will remain just what you are" (2:1806–9). For Mephistopheles, a word is pure "trope" or rhetoric, a "devil's joke" (2:2321); genuine transformation is impossible.

It is this genuine transformation which Goethe is unable to see in the French Revolution. In the "Witch's Kitchen" scene of part 1, he presents the revolution in terms of allegory. Three apes performing a slapstick routine involving a large sphere (the World) and a crown (which they break in half) mime, in the words of John R. Williams, "a satirical allegory reflecting the momentous historical events that coincided precisely with the composition of the scene," namely the

French Revolution. The "flawed Crown that breaks in two is an allusion to the precarious monarchy of France and the 'sweat and blood' with which the animals urge 'King' Mephisto to weld it together might well refer to the taxation and repression by means of which the regime tardily attempted to shore itself up."[5] What Goethe presents in this deliberately domestic "Witch's Kitchen" scene is an allegory of the "galvanic" motions of false magic – the trite spell-binding incantation, the parody of a Eucharistic revival (in Faust's ritualistic reception of chalice and potion), and the subsequent transformation of an aged and superannuated Faust into a lusty and lustful young man who sees in every woman a Helen of Troy (2:2604). All these emphasize the abortive superficiality of this early Faustian allegory.

Part I is an indictment of the limits of allegory; the Mephisthophelean word can be no more than a galvanized fragment. Like the Witch's Kitchen, it can only produce short-term and galvanic substitution, much like Faust's delusive and self-serving seduction of Gretchen. Goethe emphasizes the "galvanic" nature of Faust's seduction by associating it with lust and money. The initial courtship, for example, is made to transpire almost exclusively in terms of wealth. Mephistopheles places before Gretchen Faust's emissary of love – a treasure casket. Gretchen's initial experience of love takes her out of the realm of natural economy and places her in a position of unnatural abstraction. She is placed in a "separate" existence when she is made into a "money economy" by Faust's treasure gifts. Unable to wear her ear-rings in public, she is urged by friend Martha to wear them in private, before a mirror (2:2883–90). Abstracted into an exchange value, alienated from her material existence, Gretchen becomes the allegorical word made "transcendent" by the market imperatives of money relationship. Gretchen, immersed in the logic of general equivalence, becomes a displaced substitute, phantom proxy of the "real thing," a situation which Goethe highlights in her return as a spectral other in Walpurgis' Night (2:4190–4).

Yet Goethe is resistant to such an easy, allegorical accommodation of Gretchen. Indeed Mephistopheles' facile reading of her as an illusion is conflated with Valentine's denunciation of her as a dishonoured "whore" (2:3730). Both are willing to see in her the logic of general equivalence because neither can get beyond the confines of market imperatives. That Gretchen is redeemed from eternal damnation indicates Goethe's own resistance to marking her an allegory of allegories. She is saved because she chooses not to be delivered from death by magic (Mephistopheles) but by genuine repentance (2:4605–12). Her reappearance at the end of part II as a penitent who has gained entrance into the heavenly kingdom and who is now ready to initiate Faust's soul into the divine mystery underscores Goethe's insistence on genuine motivation in salvation and his resistance to the Gretchen episode as an easy parable of Faust's early exchanges. In short, what Mephistopheles considers only as promissory repayment of debt (the binding contractual obligations implicit in the written word) becomes, in the cases of Gretchen and Faust, the "inward co-agency" (to use Coleridge's term) of genuine redemption which absolves the participants from all contractual obligations. The Faustian exchange, therefore, pivots from a devil's joke to a joke on the Devil, and Mephistopheles becomes the "butt" of his own abortive "written word." He calls the reversal a "great investment" (2:11, 837) wasted by "vulgar lust, erotic silliness" (2:11, 838), that is, by his own willingness to be seduced by the literal word, which, in this final scene, assumes the form of advancing cherubs. Mephistopheles falls passionately into "lust"; he is defeated by his own allegorical disposition when his body literally burns with the fires of passion (2:11, 785). Part II ends with Mephistophles turning into a literal volcano, a word consumed by its own abstraction.

The volcanic impetus behind an abstracted sign is a major motif in part II. The conflation of volcanic activity, paper currency, and galvanic changes (as opposed to genuine transformation) is presented full-scale in the imperial scenes of act I, part II. Here, a depleted imperial reserve is made to be the basis of paper currency whose circulation produces delusory reprieve from a failing economy. Mephistopheles' plan to defer bankruptcy with promissory notes actually intensifies the inflationary spiral of an economy dominated by the logic of general equivalence. As the Intendant of the Treasury claims, "every one's scraping, digging and amassing, / and still our coffers are unfilled" (2:4850–1). This paradox is generated by the severance of a money economy from the material condition of the people. In the words of the Lord Steward, "the cooks are suffering no shortage; / wild boars, and stags and does, and hares, / chickens and turkeys, geese and ducks – / payments in kind – are income we are sure of/and by and large arrive on time" (2:4856–60). The problem is therefore not caused by a depletion of commodities but by a depletion of money: "I'm now supposed to pay the bills and wages / but can expect no money from the money lenders / who execute agreements that eat up / what future years must yet produce" (2:4869–72). It is the shortage of money, not goods, that has aggravated the "hypothecated" (2:4874) nature of their crisis. Unlike former times, when they could live comfortably on the supply and demand of a barter economy, the nation is now hindered by a "cash-flow" obstruction in an economy ruptured by the economics of the "hypothecated" word. Mephistopheles' paper currency is an extension of this "hypothecated" word inasmuch as Faust's wager is a corollary to this theme.

According to Marc Shell in *Money, Language, and Thought*, "Faust makes a hypothec, or hypothical deposit, of his soul in return for a still undefined power, and Mephistopheles gambles that he can give Faust the ... rest for which, it seems to Mephistopheles, Faust yearns." Shell reads the plot of *Faust* as a generation of the hypothecated word: "The plot (hupothēsis) of *Faust* contains many such additional deposits – hypothetical hypothecs – which seem to move the plot forward. Its moving force is the prompter (hupothētēs) Mephistopheles, who enables Faust to progress by a kind of spiritual or intellectual hypothesization." Shell's argument is brilliant and serves to emphasize the significance of credit and credibility in Mephistopheles' deployment of paper funds: "Mephistopheles insinuates himself into the court of the economically pressed empire and cleverly directs the courtiers' attention away from their thesaural problem, the lack of goods and specie to pay off their debts, to a fiduciary solution, a dependency on a new kind of credit. He argues that the Emperor can pay off his creditors (Gläubiger) merely by being believed."[6] It is this insidious exploitation of credit and credibility that informs the masquerade scenes; implicit in the staging of the Mephistophelean "cure" is Goethe's distinction between the inflated and the real, the allegory and the symbol.

The conflation of volcanic activity, paper currency and language becomes the central activity of the "Great Hall" scene in which a carnival masquerade presented at court takes on strong economic and linguistic dimensions. In his essay on "Symbolism," Goethe associates money with words:

Neither things nor ourselves find full expression in our words.

Something like a new world is created through language, one consisting of the essential and the incidental.

Verba valent sicut numi [words are as valuable as money]. But there are different sorts of money: gold, silver, and copper coins, or paper money. The coins are real to a degree; the paper money is only convention.

We get by in life with our everyday language, for we describe only superficial relationships. The instant we speak of deeper relationships, another language springs up: poetic language. (*Works*, 12:26)

Goethe's distinction between a superficial, inflated language and genuine poetic language emerges in the masquerade as a distinction between the allegorical and the symbolic. The artificiality of jaded art can be seen in the commercialism of the flower girls whose "wares" (2:5116) are displayed in baskets borne on their heads. The general commotion of haggling and buying contributes to an atmosphere of merchantry that is strongly associated with "popular" literature, dominated by market imperatives. Thus, flower girls and gardeners display their wares for sale in the same spirit as the Mother who enters the market proceedings by decking her daughter up for sale; "if you spread your lap, my dear," she advises her daughter, "surely you can catch one [a husband]" (2:5197–8). At this point, the Herald ushers in various poets who march out with wares of their own. In this atmosphere of competition and "haggling," the Herald summons and explains the "allegories," figures from Greek mythology arranged in pageants whose display points to a particular "truth." The first allegory of Fear, Hope and Prudence points to the significance of Prudence as handmaid to Victory. She keeps Fear and Hope in fetters, thus allowing Victory to use her power. The Herald's function is to "expound these figures' meaning" (2:5507) and to ensure the audience's satisfaction by providing protection against anything "harmful" that should get in "and spoil [their] revels" (2:5499). The spectacular displays of these pageants reinforce the idea that language under the dominion of market imperatives takes on the dimension of "huckster wares"; these are the "readerly" texts of popular sanction and commercial interests. It is ironic therefore that the Herald who so readily transmutes the "allegories" into their comprehended meaning, is "helpless to explain" (2:5509) the pageant of the Young Charioteer, even though the latter presents himself as a transparent text:

> Herald, come! continue custom
> and, before we rush away,
> draw our picture, tell our names –
> after all, we're allegories,
> and you therefore ought to know us. (2:5528–32)

In the Herald's helplessness, Goethe insinuates the distinction between an easy or facile accommodation of the text and a genuine reading of an irreconcilable text. If, in the first allegory (Faith, Hope, and Prudence), he has presented a pageant that is wholly transparent, in the second one (the Young Charioteer) he has presented his audience with what can be called a "phantasmagory."

In the pageant of the Young Charioteer and Plutus, Goethe presents us with an "allegory" which demands more than a cursory reading. This he does by "investing" his figures with significance beyond their "allegorical" status; that is, he doubles their apparent signification so that the allegory resists being a mere allegory and achieves the manifold, obscure, and irreconcilable "phantasmagory" of Coleridge's symbol. Thus the Young Charioteer is Spendthrift Poetry in a double sense – in the sense of a language which has squandered its rhetoric and in the sense of a language which seeks wealth (substance) in spirit. The former sense is given to us in the two early "demonstrations" of the Young Charioteer. In the first demonstration, the Young Charioteer snaps his fingers and immediately "rarest jewels" magically appear in mid-air. The crowd immediately "reach and grab" (2:5590) these "treasures," which turn out to be "fool's gold": "his gift takes wing and flies away; / the string of pearls breaks in his hand / and she's left holding wriggling beetles" (2:5597–9). In the second demonstration, the Young Charioteer provides a mock "laying" of pentecostal tongues; the "spark" he imparts skips from head to head, but it provides only the incandescence of a "short-lived flame" (2:5636).

A cursory reading of the Young Charioteer would assign him the role of an allegory of allegories; his readability is demonstrated in the readiness of the crowd to credit his performances with substance. But he remains a hypothecated word only to the extent that the crowd is willing to "pledge" his trope with value. It is thus that the Young Charioteer glosses over his first "trickery" with an allusion to the Herald's limitation: "it is not a herald's courtly duty / to fathom what may lie beneath their surface – / for that a keener eye is needed" (2:5607–9). The Herald's position as a limited reader parallels the position of Poetry (in the first part of the pageant) as hypothecated word. The "keener eye" emerges in the second half of the pageant when Plutus, after naming Poetry his son, dismisses him: "Now that you're rid of what encumbered you, / are wholly free, be off to your own realm!" (2:5689–90). He releases Poetry from this "wild confusion / of motley and grotesque inventions" (2:5691–2) to a realm of "clarity perceived with clarity" (2:5693) where Poetry remains unconditional, for it is a place "where you owe allegiance to yourself" (2:5694). In Plutus's dismissal of the Young Charioteer, Goethe complicates the significance of Poetry. He remains not merely a superficial language which has squandered itself in rhetoric, but becomes a linguistic agency of abundance, predicated on the poet's release from economic motives: "where I am, all men feel rich, / although, perplexed by life, they often wonder / if they should consecrate themselves to you [Plutus] or me [Poetry]" (2:5700–2). Poetry is the son of Wealth, therefore, in a double sense – as a pursuer of allegorical substance in popular texts and as a symbolic agency of genuine redemption. The dual role assigned to Poetry suggests that the word itself is the pivotal point of the wager: it is the word which "damns" or redeems us. This double exposure of the wager is the central strategy of Goethe's masque and, as we shall see later, the predominant characteristic of Carlyle's Gothic voice.

The doubleness associated with Poetry can be seen, moreover, in Plutus. Sir Greed, who accompanies Plutus, is an allegory of wealth in its most usurious sense; but in liberating his treasure-chest from its "fetters" (2:5709), Plutus points beyond his position as an allegory of wealth. He is money only to the extent that the perceiver demands that he be money; his significance *can* lie beyond the reach of a haggling and commercial crowd. It is this idea which informs the display of the volcanic gold. Taking the Herald's staff, Plutus smites the treasure chest; immediately "blood-red, / in brazen pots," gold (like volcanic lava) "surges up" (2:5711–12). The crowd, too ready to perceive trope as substance, "grab" at the "hollow illusions randomly" (2:5735–6). Plutus, "to put this mob to rout" (2:5738), uses the Herald's staff to transform the gold to flames (2:5744). Burned and stung, the mob retreats. At this point, Sir Greed steps forth and attempts to convert the lava-gold to something "good to see or eat" (2:5770) in order to "[pick] up a girl" (2:5774). His rationale is that since "gold can be converted into anything," he'll "use this metal just like clay" (2:5781–2). Sir Greed's attempt at the logic of general equivalence succeeds only too well, for the gold he kneads "becomes quite slack / and stays a shapeless mass / no matter how he molds and pummels it" (2:5786–8). His gold cannot be shaped because, dominated by the logic of general equivalence, he is unable to move beyond an understanding of gold as substance to an understanding of gold as trope. Liberated from the "fetters" of the treasure-chest, Plutean-gold can be understood only within the dynamics of the symbol. Sir Greed's "buffoonery" (2:5799) becomes testimony of a language unable to redeem itself because it has "squandered" itself in the rhetoric of general equivalence.

Even the Herald assumes a dual role by the end of the masquerade. At the beginning of the Great Hall scene, his function is restricted solely to that of appeasement; his staff dissolves the Spirit of Negation (2:5473–80); he transmutes the allegories into containable and comprehensible terms. His staff, at first an agency of allegory, becomes an agency of liberation when Plutus uses it to smite open the treasure chest and when the Herald uses it to expel Sir Greed from the pageant. It is in the final section of the pageant – in the

Great Pan episode – that the double roles of Plutus and Sir Herald become most obvious.

Here, we have, enacted in Masque form, an abortive Faustian sale. The Great God Pan, addressed as the "cosmic All" (2:5875), enters with a group of wild men to mine the lava-gold. The Great God Pan, as the sovereign signifier, marches in to lay claim to the "fountain-head" of gold, the origin of substance in discourse. But what transpires is not the eruption of gold, but volcanic fire. In an explosion prefiguring Carlyle's Cagliostro, the Great God Pan and his crew are "trapped in [a] sea of fire" and "all of this group of masqueraders burn to death" (2:5941–3); the Faustian sale ends with an "imperial magnificence" turned into "an ash-heap" overnight (2:5968–9). In a reversal reminiscent of the Jonsonian anti-masque,[7] the "artificiality" of the masqueraders is unmasked. What is more, Goethe has unmasked the "masque" as an invalid form of sovereign signification. In *The Jonsonian Masque*, Stephen Orgel points to the masque as an implicitly "loaded" wager *for* the King. The fiction generated by the court masque "is that a game of chess is taking place, and the work thus contains adversaries and a central action. But chance has been defeated – the dice are loaded, and the prince always wins ... The sovereign wins, the masque says, because it is his nature to win; and this concept of the nature of the monarch is, in one form or another, at the root of every court masque."[8] The unmasking of the Great God Pan is an unmasking of the allegorical imperatives behind such a contractual wager. This unmasking takes the form of purifying fire. The volcanic activity of this pageant, which becomes in *The French Revolution* a Carlylean trademark, is actually a powerful Goethean metaphor for the return of the repressed. Plutus warns the Herald of the "utter horror" (2:5917) which will ensue, a horror he also advises the Herald not to interrupt (2:5915). The Gothic tale of reversal which ensues is "Necessity," to use a Carlylean term, because Gothicism is a necessary corollary to the allegorical text and the betrayal of writing can be effected only by a "hypothecated" word. The Great God Pan, logic of cosmic equivalence, is one such word. The isolation of Plutus and Sir Herald from the "utter horror" of the hypothecated text suggests that Goethe intends them to be seen in this masque as non-allegorical agencies of redemption.

Goethe's conflation of volcanic activity with the Mephistophelean Spirit of Negation, however, remains a central motif in the latter part of part II. In act IV, Faust steps forth from the cloud into the rugged peaks of a mountain where he watches the cloud transmute itself into a "gigantic, yet still godlike" (2:10049) form of Helen: "Like distant icy masses/piled high upon each other, there in the east it stays,/a dazzling symbol of these fleeting days' vast import" (2:10052–4). Clouds and mountain peaks are conflated into a symbol of transcendence. Mephistopheles, however, plunges the scene into a "descendental" vision. He calls the peak "hideous maws of rock" (2:10070) and proceeds to account for them in typically Mephistophelean terms. The peaks, he tells Faust, are not really peaks at all; they once "paved the floor of hell" (2:10072) and what we on earth see as mountain peaks are actually an inverted hell "bottomed" out, as it were, by sulphuric fumes:

> What we see now is upside down
> the bottom's now become the top –
> this is the basis of those glorious doctrines
> that turn all values topsy-turvy. (2:10086–9)

Faust, however, refuses to accept Mephistopheles' "volcanic" explanation of the serrated peaks. Nature, he claims, creates the globe "complete and perfect" (2:10098) and perfection comprehends peaks and abysses, mountains and valleys (2:10099–102). The mountain peak, therefore, remains for him a symbol of the transcendent Faustian act, an "exchange" and not delusion or "theft" (2:11371). Faust's insistence on this difference is articulated most vividly in the Baucis-Philemon episode.

In this final episode, Faust's desire to harness the "aimless strength of elemental forces" to "new heights" (2:10219–20) is transmuted into his transformation of stagnant marshlands into a second Eden (2:11560–70). To complete this task, he yearns for the linden trees which still remain in the hands of the elderly couple, Baucis and Philemon:

> Among their branches I would like to build
> a platform with a panoramic vista
> and so obtain an unobstructed view
> of all that I have now accomplished –
> survey with one inclusive look
> this masterpiece the human spirit has wrought
> to augment, by intelligent planning,
> the space its peoples have for living. (2:11243–50)

The linden trees, commanding a panoramic view of Faust's reclaimed land, would have been an apt symbol of Faustian achievement. What Faust desires in exchange, however, is translated into Mephistophelean plunder. Mephistopheles, with the help of his mighty men, raids the hut of the elderly couple and literally steals ownership. This discrepancy between Faustian Act and Mephistophelean Plunder becomes crucial in the final scene when Faust, blinded by Care, hastens the fulfilment of his plans (2:11501). Summoning his workmen, he prompts them to complete the task he has begun. Mephistopheles, taking advantage of a blinded Faust, summons his lemures and, instead of completing the Faustian plan, orders the lemures to dig Faust's grave. Committed to the logic of general equivalence, Mephistopheles expects an easy "plunder" of Faust's soul – "It falls, and all is finished" (2:11596) – but this facile ending is transmuted into an abortive "investment" (2:11837) when Faust's soul is redeemed by the Heavenly Host.

The volcanic impetus of Mephistopheles remains, for Goethe, untenable; in the "Classical Walpurgis' Night" scene of part II, Anaxagoris' claim to eminence (the creation of an almost instant mountain from volcanic eruption) is defeated by Thales' revelation that this eminence is "make-believe" (2:7946). Goethe is wary of instant and facile solutions. Events like "Nature's living fluxes / have never counted days and nights and hours" (2:7861–2), and performances which disregard the labour of time and effort are suspect. In one of his maxims, Goethe reflects: "Throughout the history of scientific investigation we find observers leaping too quickly from phenomenon to theory; hence, they fall short of the mark and become theoretical" (*Works*, 12:308). Mephistopheles is one such theorist; his "volcanic" theory is as reductive as the "one-eyed" vision of the Phorkyads. Sharing one eye and tooth, the three sisters are an embodiment of the language of general equivalence. Mephistopheles becomes an extension of this monstrous trinity when he borrows the "likeness of the third" (2:8017) Phorkyad and assumes the identity of Phorkyas. Mephistopheles, in disguise, assumes the role of the ancient stewardess of Menelaus's wealth and possessions. Her two-dimensionality is reflected in her eagerness to carry out Menelaus's orders to sacrifice Helen and in her ready condemnation of Helen's elopement:

> The man who stays at home to guard his precious wealth,
> who takes good care to caulk his house's lofty walls
> and to secure its roof against the rain's assault,
> will know prosperity however long he live;
> but he who lightly steps with hasty foot across
> his threshold's sacred limit, heedless of all law,
> on his return may well still find the same old place,
> but all things altered, even if not all destroyed. (2:8974–81)

Conservative of wealth and possessions, loyal to the old master Menelaus, Phorkyas is the manifestation of a superannuated classicism, an ideal that is now exhausted and in need of revival. The revival comes in the return of Helen, whose doubled consciousness (2:8872) marks the beginning of genuine transformation. Her dissociation from a superannuated classicism can be seen in act III when Lynceus, the watchman, places her beyond the language of general equivalence: "our lives and wealth now are / subject to her beauty's power" (2:9348–9). Helen's beauty is unconditional; it transcends wealth, the measure of Menelaus's power. Thus, before Helen, Lynceus can only say: "Set against such loveliness / all is empty nothingness" (2:9354–5).

Menelaus' fortified classicism can be revived only by love. The union of Faust and Helen takes place in a second Eden – an Arcadian "domain of ever-youthful vigor" (2:9568) which displaces the "mighty fortress" (2:9566) of an antiquated Classicism and then revives it by means of the trinity of Faust, Helen, and son Euphorion, whose language, unlike that of the Phorkyads, seeks transmutation by the genuinely symbolic. Euphorion is the symbol of unceasing activity: "I can't bear to have / what's easily gained / only what's conquered / affords true delight" (2:9781–4). His parallel to the "classical" Icarus doubles his significance; unlike Icarus's, Euphorion's fall is not defeat but release. Goethe is emphatic that Euphorion's flight is sustained, if only for a short time: *"He flings himself into the air. For a moment his garments support him and his head radiates light – a luminous trail follows him"* (stage direction following 2:9900). Euphorion's apotheosis transmutes a tragic signifier into symbolic affirmation. The Chorus's final words – "All that is transitory / is only a symbol; / what seems unachievable / here is seen done" (2:12104–7) – bear testimony to the unceasing necessity of change and incarnation. If the monstrous trinity of the Phorkyads resists change, the trinity of Faust-Helen-Euphorion is the living incarnation of it.

Goethe's insistence on the necessity of change is made emphatic by his use of an economics of terror. An allegorical language "terrifies" because it is unable to move beyond the "economics" of the word to an "economy" of dialectical regeneration. The Gothic voice is therefore a necessary corollary to the allegory.

While *Faust* impressed Carlyle with this "machinery" for an economics of terror, *The Monk* and *Melmoth the Wanderer* left him with the recognition that such machinery can be deployed only within a "Gothic" tale of reversal. If the Gothic voice is the dying gasp of a superannuated language, its articulation is the unmasking of its own fiction. In *The Monk*, for example, the self-consuming logic of a superannuated system is the prime catalyst of this unmasking. At the basis of this system is a "money" economy, an attempt to reduce the soul to an equivalent term; monasticism, the sanctuary of spiritual wealth, becomes ironically a repository of political power. The soul, materialized into an equivalent value, assumes the burden of allegory: thus it is that Ambrosio insists on his position as transcendental signifier; he is the "Man of Holiness" who seems destined for holy and monastic life. Left as a babe before the monastery door, Ambrosio becomes the language of monasticism itself; pure, virginal, saintly. "In the course of his life, he has never been known to transgress a simple rule of his order; the smallest stain is not to be discovered in his character."[9] Dominated by the logic of general equivalence, Ambrosio forgets the human dimensions of "sinning." His rejection of Agnes's plea for compassion is a case in point. Unable to accept the unconditional nature of human frailty, Ambrosio refuses to intercede on her behalf. Agnes's severe punishment under the hands of the convent prioress is the unmasking of a rigid and persecuting system. By sacrificing Agnes to the logic of equivalence, Ambrosio becomes a copy of his own grandfather, who, also dominated by the necessity of "ancestral" equivalence, has conveniently "forgotten" his grandson in the monastery. Himself a pawn in the feud between mother and grandfather, Ambrosio is the unknown element suppressed in the name of familial integrity. His return at the end, in the form of outrageous crimes – the rape of his sister and murder of his mother – constitutes the vengeance of the repressed.

The monastic order fails because it has misread the legacy of Christ. Grounded in the logistics of the wager, monasticism participates in the idiom of purchase: if I sacrifice myself body and soul to heavenly devotion, I will purchase a spot in the heavenly kingdom. Accessibility to the heavenly kingdom is based on a contractual agreement between reader and sign. Ambrosio's reading of the monastic text is based on the acceptance of this contractual agreement: as long as he refrains from invoking the name of Satan or revoking his contract with God, he remains secure in his salvation. Thus, when Matilda urges him to "employ hell's agency" to secure the rape of Antonia, Ambrosio refuses on the ground that a conscious alliance with God's enemy will revoke his previous contract with God (266). Yet, he willingly concedes to the use of "human means" (267) to violate Antonia. As salvation is understood only in terms of contractual obligations, Ambrosio sees little necessity for genuine repentance. The same myopic obsession with the binding nature of words motivates his final "contract" with the fiend. Fearful of his execution, Ambrosio signs the parchment with the understanding that he will be "saved" from the Inquisition. The contract "saves" him – but only to the *letter* of the word; leaving him to die in the mountains, the fiend explains the "forgotten" clause: "Our contract? Have I not performed my part? What more did I promise than to save you from your prison? Have I not done so? Are you not safe from the Inquisition – safe from all but from me? Fool that you were to confide yourself to a devil! Why did you not stipulate for life, and power, and pleasure? Then all would have been granted: now, your reflections come too late. Miscreant, prepare for death ... " (419). The final irony resides in Ambrosio's recognition that what he has valued in the name of the contract betrays too well in the letter of the word. He is betrayed by the monastic text even as he himself is the text that has betrayed its readers.

The same betrayal of reader by text occurs in *Melmoth the Wanderer*. Here, the reading of an old manuscript initiates entrance into a diseased world. The contractual obligations of reading and the breaking of these obligations become the structural principle of a text aimed at deflating the Catholic doctrine of salvation as contractual bargains made with God. Salvation as contractual wager becomes the pivotal point of Maturin's Gothic narrative: as each character reads, he enters into a contractual agreement which irrevocably defaults; reading initiates a series of narrative exchanges which, instead of fulfilling the contractual obligations of comprehensibility and accessibility, plunges the reader into the unknown; in effect, the deficit (the series of unknowns) accumulated in the narrative is produced by reading and the debt accrued by the reader is discharged only in the final segment of the novel.

Maturin deploys an economics of terror which is best understood in terms of his anti-papist sentiments. For him, the Catholic Church (specifically in the form of the Inquisition) is a superannuated allegory. Burdened by the tyranny of wealth and tradition, the Church secures its survival through the logistics of the bargain. When salvation is promised to those willing to pay the price, the system remains intact by general subscription. Those unwilling to pay the price are destroyed; because salvation is predicated on their willingness to enter the bargain, their unwillingness to do so ensures their destruction. This suppression of heretical behaviour remains the central strategy of the Inquisition. In the conditional universe of general equivalence, the elimination of difference is crucial: it ensures the validity of the conditional term; by extension, it guarantees the logic of the bargain. The Catholic Church, therefore, becomes no more than a self-ingesting tautology, a mother that feeds on her own children. The cannibalism inherent in the doctrinal legacy of the Church is manifested in *The Monk* in Ambrosio's rape and destruction of his own sister. In Maturin's *Melmoth the Wanderer*, it is reflected in the miscreant parricide whose pursuit of general equivalence necessitates the gruesome murder of his own sister and her lover. His recounting of the lovers' demise slowly divests love of its illusion. The final vision of the starved young man feeding on his beloved's breast puts a cruel twist to a tale of love:[10] stripped of their tender prerogatives, the lovers, like the voyeuristic brother feeding on the agonies of his own sister, become no better than Blake's self-ingesting primates. Gesture without spirit, body without soul, the parricide remains the strongest testimony against a superannuated Church. Reflecting on the callousness of the parricide, Monçado remarks:

This *union of antipodes*, this unnatural alliance of the extremes of guilt and light-mindedness, I had never met or imagined before. He started from the visions of a parricide, and sung songs that would have made a harlot blush. How ignorant of life I must have been, not to know that guilt and insensibility often join to tenant and deface the same mansion, and that there is not a more strong and indissoluble alliance on earth, than that between the hand that dare do anything, and the heart that can feel nothing. (202–3)

The parricide, bringing together the hand that dares anything and the heart that feels nothing, illustrates most brutally the logic of Coleridge's allegory.

Monçado's own situation in the monastery participates in the idiom of purchase. Left in the monastery as atonement for his mother's sins, he is the pawn in a contractual bargain between his mother and God. That the logistics of the bargain are not only promoted but effected through the director of the monastery places the Church in more than questionable straits. The reduction of Monçado to an unmotivated sign is further indictment against conventual life. Like his mother's magnificent dress, whose spread on the stone floor prevents his escape from the monastery (99), Monçado is transformed into a Gothic allegory: he is a signifier without signified. His mechanical presence both sustains and infects the monastic legacy; thus, while his stupor makes a case for a repentant monk, it also unsettles the monastic conscience. Monçado's automaton gestures, the monks argue, make a "mockery" of conventual life (100). An agency of exposure, Monçado's presence haunts the cloister like a forgotten self.

In his attempt to escape from the cloister, Monçado purchases the service of the parricide. Misreading the latter as one who can easily be "bought," Monçado discovers the truth, just at the point of escape – that while gold has been lucrative enough for the criminal, what proves more seductive is a "higher bribe": "Your brother gave gold," admits the parricide, "but the convent promised me salvation" (220). Monçado's wager defaults because it has been superseded by a more promising contract; he fails because his saviour is part and parcel of a tautological system which sells salvation at the price of treachery: "Every offender may purchase his immunity by consenting to become the executioner of the offender whom he betrays and denounces" (224). This idea of the Church as allegory is reinforced in the latter part of Monçado's tale, in the persecution of heretics by members of the Inquisition and in the subsequent rebellion of the people against the Inquisitors.

In the procession of the ecclesiastical orders of Madrid, Maturin recreates the "double exposure" of Goethe's Great Hall Masque. It is interesting to note that both Lewis and Maturin have accommodated in some way Goethe's use of the masque in *Faust*, which in many ways can be seen as revision of a conventional form. Reversing the structure of the Jonsonian masque, Goethe ends his masquerade with the unmasking of a royal procession. His Great God Pan is unmasked as a hollow signifier and the pageant which began with the pomp and circumstance of the royal prerogative ends in a great "ashheap." Lewis and Maturin (and Carlyle as well) have assimilated this procession-turned-riot into their Gothic narratives. In *The Monk*, the pilgrimage processional turns into mob violence when Mother St Ursula exposes the Prioress as a "monastic tyrant" (*Monk*, 339). The mob violence and conflagration become the means of purification when the convent, site of deception and hypocrisy, is consumed by flames. Similarly, Maturin recreates in the ecclesiastical procession a proclamation of general equivalence. Monçado, watching the pageantry from the highest apartment of the Jew's house, is ironically overwhelmed by the awe-inspiring power of a procession in full regalia. A victim of the Inquisition, he is "caught up" in the "awful inscription" of the Inquisitors: "It was a sight to convert all hearts, and I exulted I was a Catholic" (*Melmoth*, 253). Caught up in a "general will," the "one and indivisible" ecclesiastical republic, Monçado echoes the "cosmic" significance of the Great God Pan. His euphoria, like Pan's, is short-lived, for adulation quickly changes into execution when the crowd, discovering the presence of a parricide in the processional retinue, unmasks the hypocrisy of a superannuated institution.

This unmasking of pretension becomes, as we shall see later, a central Carlylean strategy in *The French Revolution*. Suffice it to say that Goethe's processional masque has allowed for full deployment of an economics of terror. Ostensibly a language of equivalence, the procession is sign of a contracted bargain. Monçado's exultation at being a "Catholic" is testimony of the persuasiveness implicit in the language of pageantry. He too becomes part of a bargained salvation. The bargain-turned-deficit is, however, corollary to this equation.

With this corollary in mind, we can perhaps better understand the position of the Wanderer in Maturin's novel. More Mephistophelean than Faustian, the Wanderer occupies the pages of the work as an indictment not so much of pacts with Satan as of pacts with God. Indeed his position as tempter serves only to reinforce the vision of human perseverance and good, for not one of his victims is willing to bargain his soul for exemption from pain; not one of his victims is willing to accept the Wanderer's offer for substitution. If anything at all, the Wanderer reinforces the brutality of monied interests, since these victims are, more often than not, brought to their despair by the economics of the word. Immalee, for example, is brought to the Wanderer's hand by her parents' subscription to wealth; the Guzmans are brought to the edge of destruction by mercenary ecclesiastics; Elinor is victimized by the avarice of Mrs Sandal. As Charles Baldick states in the introduction to Maturin's text: "It is money, after all, that sets this story in motion, from John Melmoth's first arrival at his rich uncle's deathbed to the fatal inheritance which ruins the Mortimers in 'The Lovers' Tale.' More particularly, it is family wealth which repeatedly brings disaster to the novel's leading characters" (xviii). The Wanderer, like Goethe's Mephistopheles, is a criticism of the allegorical text.

Despite Carlyle's criticism of Gothic romances, he has read enough of the genre to understand the machinery of Gothic conventions. As Mark Cumming explains: "Although [Carlyle's] letter amply reveals Carlyle's contempt for the excesses of romance, it inevitably reflects his attraction to the form, and we would not be unkind to enquire, why Carlyle, given his 'profound indifference,' should have stayed up until midnight, let alone four in the morning, [to complete his reading of Lewis' *The Monk*]."[11] Attracted to the irony implicit in Gothic fiction, conscious of the machinery of the wager such fiction exploits, Carlyle has not so much rejected Gothicism itself as reinvented it within the context of historical discourse. He has not so much rejected the insipid sensationalism of Lewis's *The Monk* as reinvested its economics of terror within new, historical idiom. Cumming concludes: "For Carlyle, the roles of myopic rationalist and unyielding moralist are not comfortable ones: his desire is less to banish the specters, the ass-eared giants and the goblin barbers –

they do reappear for him, at the most incongruous times, in the persons of kings, *philosophes* and revolutionaries – than to accommodate them in some form consistent with his fact-centred aesthetic."[12] This attempt at revisioning can be seen in his experimental narrative, "The Diamond Necklace," which puts the machinery of the wager to unconstitutional but productive use.

Written as a reconstruction of an "actual Transaction" (W, 28:330), "The Diamond Necklace" incorporates as its framework the dialectics of truth and fiction. Maintaining in the opening section that "Romance exists" in "Reality alone" (W, 28:329), Carlyle attempts in his narrative what Cagliostro proclaims to be the "*marrying* of Truth and Sham" (W, 28:394). This marriage indeed is the basis of Carlyle's Gothicism. If "Narrative is *linear*" and "Action is *solid*" (W, 27:89), then the writer has the responsibility to narrate in a way which would allow him to "paint [the transaction] truly" (W, 28:330) rather than reduce it to a "wretched politico-metaphysical Abstraction" (W, 28:326). Carlyle's Gothicism is a strategy of double exposure. It assimilates from all three Faustian analogues the logistics of the wager; it inherits from Goethe the rubric of the masquerade; it inherits from Maturin the betrayal of the text.

The diamond necklace which Boehmer has "arranged and agglomerated" (W, 28:332) is an emblem of the wager itself, a signifier invested with the idiom of money economy. The necklace is not "made" (in the sense of being created), so claims Carlyle, but "enlisted under Boehmer's flag, – made to take rank and file, in new order" (W, 28:333) like a newly agglomerated republic, trading in lives for a new badge of patriotic fervour. A "sovereign signifier," the necklace is "put together" into a dumb idol which Boehmer and Cardinal Rohan misread within the idiom of purchase. Boehmer reads the necklace as a "talismanic *Sesame*" (W, 28:331) to royal favour; Rohan reads it as a wager to reclaim a lost paradise (W, 28:346). Both are dominated by the "fixed idea," Carlyle's epithet for the allegorical text. "[B]eware of fixed ideas" (W, 28:349), writes Carlyle, for men of fixed ideas are foolish men: "They sell their Inheritance ... though it is a Paradise, for a crotchet" (W, 28:348). A transaction of supernal and infernal dimensions, the diamond necklace is the signifier suspended between two possible readings – the miraculous symbol, "translucent between [reader and writer]; transfigured, lifted up into the serene of Universal-History" (W, 28:330) or the "ill-starred" allegory, "[pendulating] between Heaven and Earth, a thing rejected of *both*" (W, 28:395). For Carlyle, it is the Gothic imperative which can divest the necklace of illusion, for it is in the return of the repressed that the masquerade is exposed as a sham.

This unmasking of the masquerade is maintained throughout the narrative by means of a mock-heroic tone. In the presentation of the Queen at the "Oeil de Boeuf," Carlyle insists on invading the gallery with spectres of defeat and ruin (W, 28:382), a trail of ghostly residue which subverts Rohan's expected victory. Carlyle's insistence that the transaction is the "[disgigging]" of "Gigmanity" (W, 28:353) can be seen in his references to the fraud as a series of "Scenic Exhibitions," conducted by the dramaturgist Lamotte. Mephistophelean in impetus, Lamotte is the text whose currency is based on the hypothecated word. The "gilt-paper Autographs" (W, 28:364) she secures for Rohan remain, like the paper money in *Faust*, "hypothetical" words. Claiming descent from Henri Second, Lamotte is revealed to be the progeny of a stolen name: "She boasts herself descended by what is called *natural* generation, from the Blood-Royal of France: Henri Second, before the fatal tourney-lance entered his right eye and ended him, appears to have had, successively or simultaneously, four – unmentionable women: and so, *in vice* of the third of these, came a certain Henri de Saint-Remi into this world" (W, 28:350). With a heritage that is "stolen" and a "bastard royal life," more pretension than reality, Lamotte is the emblem of Imposture itself. Her unmasking at the end of the narrative takes on Gothic overtones: her Dramaturgical skills of deception are superseded by those of another – "Destiny" itself (W, 28:389). Like Goethe's Mephistopheles being duped by the Chorus at the end, Lamotte is further "unmasked" by the prophecies of Arch-Quack Cagliostro. Lamotte is given the nemesis of the convent prioress: hurled forth from a third-storey window, she ends her masquerade as a "mangled squelch of gore, confusion and abomination; which men huddle underground, with no burial-stone" (W, 28:397). Her nemesis is unleashed by the necessity of volcanic fire, Cagliostro's "Red Sea of Fire" whose "fire tongue" enwrapping the "World" consumes the "Empire of Imposture" (W, 28:399). The same necessity governs Rohan's and Boehmer's assimilation of the allegorical tongue: "Two fixed ideas, Cardinal's and Jeweller's, a negative and a positive, have felt each other; stimulated now by hope, are rapidly revolving round each other, and approximating; like two flames, are stretching-out long fire-tongues to join and be one" (W, 28:376). The Gothic voice implicit in this passage predicates the reversal at the end when the tongues are transformed into a final conflagration.

Rohan and Boehmer are fixed by their allegorical reading of the text. Their "reading" of the situation becomes a form of wager, a transaction; what they hope to be "transacted" in their favour through the necklace becomes the dominant legacy of the text. Thus the "gilt Autographs" circulate with a momentum dictated by Rohan's confidence in Lamotte. Two hundred such letters between the Cardinal and the Queen are said to have circulated during the "masquerade." Believing the "gilt papers" to be tokens from the Queen, Rohan responds with "charitable cash" donated "on her Majesty's behalf," advanced into the hands of the Countess. In the sense that the masquerade sustains itself on its own rhetoric, Rohan contributes to his own deception. This Carlyle emphasizes in his description of Rohan. Using the Gothic voice of double exposure, he seals Rohan's doom from the very beginning of the narrative. Rohan cannot but be deceived, for his nature is built on deception itself: "A figure thrice-clothed with honours; with plush, and civic and ecclesiastic garniture of all kinds; but in itself little other than an amorphous congeries of contradictions, somnolence and violence, foul passions and foul habits" (W, 28:341–2). Rohan is an "extraneous" (W, 28:326) text, for "it is by his plush cloaks and wrappages mainly ... that such a figure sticks together" (W, 28:342); there is nothing of the "miraculous All" (W, 28:329) in Rohan. A figure "agglomerated" like the diamond necklace, Rohan is the allegorical text most prone to betray itself. Each character in "The Diamond Necklace" is betrayed by his fixed idea, and the Gothicism which ensues can be located in the "deficit" accrued through the series of transactions. The Gothic apparatus in "The Diamond Necklace" provides Carlyle with an economics of terror which he does not fully deploy until *The French Revolution*.

3 Economics and Economy in *The French Revolution*

Carlyle's "Gothic" experiment in "The Diamond Necklace" takes on a more aggressive form in *The French Revolution*. The logistics of the wager, the betrayal of the word and the place of the reader in the text become the very means by which the political crisis in France is made not only into an allegory of economic collapse but also into a metaphor of (mis)reading. Central to this misreading is Rousseau's *Social Contract*, the political wager of "contracted" nationhood. The degeneration of this new political text into the Reign of Terror can be seen as an extension of the logic in Rohan's demise. In exposing Rohan as the allegorical text, Carlyle makes "The Diamond Necklace" into a parable of reading. Placing the "fixed" text within a money economy, Carlyle unmasks the allegorical reader as a foiled Icarus (W, 28:331), a failed attempt at transcendence. But while he denounces what he deems to be a failed reader, Carlyle also inscribes the ideal reader within the text. The ideal reader is the "good reader" Carlyle frequently addresses in a tone of brotherly camaraderie; he is also the reader invoked at the end of chapter 1 as a necessary agent in the transformation of text to meaning:

For the rest, an earnest inspection, faithful endeavour has not been wanting, on our part ... Were there but on the reader's part a kindred openness, a kindred spirit of endeavour! Beshone strongly, on both sides, by such united twofold Philosophy, this poor opaque Intrigue of the *Diamond Necklace* might become quite translucent between us; transfigured, lifted up into the serene of Universal-History; and might hang there like a smallest Diamond Constellation, visible without telescope, – so long as it could. (W, 28:330)

Unlike the allegorical reader who consumes the text, the ideal reader "transfigures" it into a diamond constellation. What might have remained "opaque" to the allegorical reader is transformed into something quite "translucent between [author and reader]," a transformation which suggests not so much an easy reduction of text to clarity as a symbiotic synthesis of meaning. Author and reader are seen as complements of a whole, the author initiating a signifying process which is not complete until the reader has synthesized some form of meaning from the signs. In this sense, Carlyle anticipates Sartre, for whom writing is an act of community: "the operation of writing implies that of reading as its dialectical correlative and these two connected acts necessitate two distinct agents. It is the joint effort of author and reader which brings upon the scene that concrete and imaginary object which is the work of the mind. There is no art except for and by others."[1] Reading as an act of community, an act of brotherhood, is the very problem "enacted" in "The Diamond Necklace." To what extent is this relationship between author and reader, forged on the basis of a money economy, a travesty of "brotherhood"? To what extent is "currency" the paradigm of an overdetermined text? And to what extent is the reader's place in such a text framed by a contractarian imperative? The diamond necklace, as emblem of the wager, anticipates the contractarian "brotherhood" of the newly constituted Republic in *The French Revolution*. Forged on the "aggregative" principle, such brotherhood is a parody of the ideal communion between author and reader which Sartre describes as an "enterprise" initiated by the author, but completed with the reader:

If I appeal to my readers so that we may carry the enterprise which I have begun to a successful conclusion, it is self-evident that I consider him as a pure freedom, as an unconditioned activity; thus, in no case can I address myself to his passiveness, that is, try to *affect* him, to communicate to him, from the very first, emotions of fear, desire, or anger. There are, doubtless, authors who concern themselves solely with arousing these emotions because they are foreseeable, manageable, and because they have at their disposal sure-fire means of provoking them.[2]

Rohan's misreading of the text is induced by his "passiveness," his willingness to be framed by the "sure-fire" tactics of allegorical writer Lamotte. His misreading is juxtaposed to the prophetic reading of the "ideal reader." At the end of "The Diamond Necklace," Carlyle points to the role this ideal reader plays in activating the text: "This little Business, like a little cloud, bodied itself forth in skies clear to the unobservant: but with such hues of deep-tinted villany [sic], dissoluteness and general delirium as, to the observant, betokened it electric; and wise men, a Goethe for example, boded Earthquakes. Has not the Earthquake come?" (W, 28:402). Against the totalitarian "brotherhood" of a "fixed idea," Carlyle posits a more legitimate brotherhood – a brotherhood of literacy based on the dyadic interaction between author and reader, by which the reader becomes the material expression of authorial prophecy. It is in this sense that reader Goethe "boded" and bodied forth earthquakes, for he could read in "this little Business" the signs of the times.

A reading brotherhood fostered on the basis of a barter economy involves the reader as a necessary expression and catalyst of the text; in the words of Tilottama Rajan, the reader becomes a necessary "supplement" to the text, recovering the separation of signifier from signified that occurs in writing. If "writing disrupts the bond between signifier and signified that exists before expression," the reader is able "to restore this link" by transforming "intention into reference and [reuniting] the signifier and signified by an act of emotional commitment."[3] Rephrased in economic terms, writing is the coining of general equivalence, the production of an arbitrary and abstracted third term, effected by the rupture of signifier from signified. The reader as supplement recuperates this abstraction by returning it to a barter economy of material expression. The reader "activates" the text by returning the displaced meaning to the word and the word becomes thing (or "symbol" for Carlyle) in an economy which bases its "brotherhood" not on the aggregative principle of a contracted wager, but on the "brotherhood" of the incarnational text – the word made flesh through the grace of the reader.

This brotherhood between reader and author necessarily makes reading a generative act. "Reading can no longer be conceived as the reconstruction of an original meaning but must be seen as the production of new meaning," Rajan writes; from this perspective, one might argue that reading participates in the economy of Coleridge's "logical opposition" when it produces an unneutralized "third term": "Reading does indeed engender signification: in the act of reading, signifier and signified are fused through a third element – involvement, or what Ricoeur calls 'appropriation.' But this fusion does not occur through a reading that reconstructs the meaning of the text and thus institutionalizes itself by making the work into a signified ... Using the text ... as a pre-text, the reader through divination generates the work."[4] Coleridge's "third term" of irreconcilable differences is the matrix for such reader participation. A reader-generated interpretation can be produced only through the non-reductive and non-neutralizing interaction between reader and author. Such generation is dependent on an ideal reader prepared not to "neutralize" the indeterminate text but to embark on what Wolfgang Iser in *The Act of Reading* calls the "wandering viewpoint,"[5] a journey a willing reader must make in order to negotiate his passage through a receding and resistant text. The journey takes not the form of a denotative transfer, but of a proleptic and retroactive synthesis. According to Iser, the reader's position in the text is never given full denotative value; rather, it is the position of Carlyle's reader who stands "at the conflux of two Eternities" (W, 2:134), straddling an uneasy accommodation of past and present. The reader's position is therefore "at the point of intersection between retention and protension. Each individual sentence correlate prefigures a particular horizon, but this is immediately transformed into the background for the next correlate and must therefore necessarily be modified ... In most literary texts ... the sequence of sentences is so structured that the correlates serve to modify and even frustrate the expectations they have aroused."[6] Iser's wandering viewpoint places unequivocal responsibility on the reader who must keep himself open to changing perspectives at all times. "Reading," writes Iser, "does not merely flow forward" because "recalled segments ... have a retroactive effect, with the present transforming the past."[7] "Thus," Iser continues, "in the time-flow of the reading process, past and future continually converge in the present moment, and the synthesizing operations of the wandering viewpoint enable the text to pass through the reader's mind as an ever-expanding network of connections."[8] It is this network that ultimately unfolds the reader's understanding of the text. Iser's analysis of the reader's role affirms the necessity of active engagement on the part of the reader. The ideal reader is one who is willing to abandon passive enlightenment for textual restructuring. The ideal reader is the one who is willing to make the text into an "event."

Indeed, Coleridge's unknown correspondent is what the ideal reader is not; unwilling to descend with Coleridge "into the dark Cave of Trophonius" (*Biographia Literaria*, 1:302), there to suffer through a dark night of the soul prior to revelation, he advises Coleridge to defer publication of his treatise on the Imagination. The reasons he supplies are transparently utilitarian: first, the additional pages will increase the expense of the work; secondly, every reader who (like himself) is resistant to the study of a "subject so abstrusely treated" will be "almost entitled to accuse [Coleridge] of a sort of imposition on him" (1:303). Sympathetic as he may seem, the unknown correspondent marks the limit of reader passivity: it is his unwillingness to take part in "kindred endeavour" which reduces the author to inaction; the result is an absent text. Unlike Carlyle's "good reader," whose kindred openness permits the work to constellate a symbol, the unknown correspondent is the neutralizing third term.

If reading is an act of community, its redemptive value lies in what Carlyle perceives to be the distinction between a brotherhood of contractual obligations and one of prophetic literacy. The former he discovers in the contractarian ideology of the "Evangelist Jean Jacques" (W, 3:145) and in the revolutionaries' furore for a National Constitution; such a "constituted" community remains allegorical at best and this Carlyle delineates through the arbitrary scenes of "discipline" of the Reign of Terror. On the other hand, the brotherhood of literacy emerges in *The French Revolution* as a form of reader-author symbiosis. Exploring the time-lapse between the death of Louis XV and the ideal reader's perception of the event, Carlyle points to the advantages of a multidimensional vision: "To the eye of History many things, in that sick-room of Louis, are now visible, which to the Courtiers there present were invisible. For indeed it is well said, 'in every object there is inexhaustible meaning; the eye sees in it what the eye brings means of seeing'" (W, 2:5). Unlike the courtiers, who can perceive only what lies immediately before them, the eye of history can read "inexhaustible meaning"; thus, the ideal reader whose "eye brings means of seeing" is beckoned to do so in his reading of the King's deathbed. Author and reader participate in a brotherhood of spirit when both bring to the moment a consciousness that is both proleptic and retroactive, when both read in the event not only a sick French king but an ailing "French Kingship" which "after long rough tear and wear, is breaking down" (W, 2:7).

Again, in his concluding address to the reader, Carlyle refers to their relationship as a sacred one – an "incarnated Word" – for while he, the author, was "but as a Voice," the reader's participation in this voice transforms the "voice" into living speech: "For whatsoever once sacred things become hollow jargons, yet while the Voice of Man speaks with Man, hast thou not there the living fountain out of which all sacrednesses sprang, and will yet spring?" Author and reader stand together, a sacred brotherhood, their "[t]oilsome ... journeying" (W, 4:323) done. Through this brotherhood of the "incarnate Word," Carlyle criticizes the contractarian brotherhood of Revolutionary ideology.

If, through author and reader, Carlyle presents us with an ideal symbiotic reading, in King Louis xv he presents us with a failed or abortive reader when he makes the King participate in a final retroactive reading of his own life. Unable to participate genuinely in the text of life, the King is the apotheosis of the passive reader. Having had the "kingliest abhorrence of Death ... He would not suffer Death to be spoken of; avoided the sight of churchyards, funereal monuments, and whatsoever could bring it to mind." The same forgetfulness marks his reluctance to deal with the hunger and suffering of his people. Confronted by the brother of a peasant who had died from hunger, "the King gave his steed the spur." The same abstracted consciousness is reflected in Carlyle's description of him as a man who has the "resource of the Ostrich" (W, 2:19). What his "moneyed" consciousness would fain forget, however, is brought to face him at his deathbed: "Unhappy man, there as thou turnest, in dull agony, on thy bed of weariness, what a thought is thine! Purgatory and Hell-fire, now all too possible, in the prospect: in the retrospect, – alas, what thing didst thou do that were not better undone; what mortal didst thou generously help ... Miserable man! thou 'hast done evil as thou couldst': thy whole existence seems one hideous abortion and mistake of Nature; the use and meaning of thee not yet known" (W, 2:20). Unable to read himself, to generate himself within a meaningful economy, King Louis stands a "Solecism Incarnate," an abortive word. His flaw is that he has done "nothing" (W, 2:21); the incarnation of a passive reader, he witnesses the passing of a feudal symbol into mere "chimera and scenic show" (W, 2:20). His whole life, read with the "formulas" of a money economy, can generate nothing beyond a self-devouring consumption: a "King Donothing" and "Eatall" (W, 2:22), King Louis, the "fabulous Griffin *devouring* the Works of Man" (W, 2:20), is himself devoured at the end. The irony is made most poignant when we see that "Louis the Unforgotten" has forgotten too much. He is finally consigned to oblivion at his funeral when he is impatiently crushed and huddled underground by his courtiers, who, "rushing as in wager, to salute the new Sovereigns" (W, 2:25), reveal their inclination to be "moneyed" readers as well.

As Carlyle leaves the King's deathbed, he pauses for a moment to extend his narration by making the ruler an emblem of reader consciousness: "Louis was a Ruler; but art not thou also one?" The deathbed scene becomes a scene of reading when each reader is exhorted not to "lay flattering unction to his [own] soul." The sins of

Louis are not confined to royalty; even the "meanest man" reading from his "narrow brickfield" (*W*, 2:20) is capable of an abortive reading. Seen from this perspective, *The French Revolution* is not so much a historicizing of a political event as an extension of the Romantic preoccupation with scenes of reading. Such scenes, according to Tilottama Rajan, are "extended *narration*[s] of the process of communication or expression." A scene points to the boundaries of conceptual statements: "A scene arises from a surplus of meaning that cannot be reduced to a conceptual statement. We narrate fundamental problems because our attempt to state them logically does not fully explain them."[9] "[A]ll action," writes Carlyle in "On History," is "by its nature, to be figured as extended in breadth and in depth, as well as in length" (*W*, 27:88). Again, in *The French Revolution*, Carlyle locates the whole purpose of the book in his search for a way to read "in some tolerably approximate way" the "event" called the French Revolution: "In general, may we not say that the French Revolution lies in the heart and head of every violent-speaking, of every violent-thinking French Man? How the Twenty-five Millions of such, in their perplexed combination, acting and counter-acting may give birth to events; which event successively is the cardinal one; and from what point of vision it may best be surveyed: this is the problem" (*W*, 2:214). The events in *The French Revolution* are narratives of representation; implicit in these narratives is the situating of the wager within a crisis of reading.

The uncrowning of the sovereign signifier brings to the fore the problem of "constituting" meaning in the text of the French regime. Once the sovereign signifier is divested of substance, where does one locate the essence of French nationhood? When the Crown is stripped of its sovereignty, where does one locate power? For the revolutionaries, the constituting of power within the wager ushers in a new model of reading. It is perhaps no coincidence that Iser refers to the reading process as "acts of constitution"[10] because the reader's role when confronted with an indeterminate text is to "constitute" meaning or "connectability." The problem with the National Constitution is its obsession with the contract or wager as a form of talismanic connection. The wager replaces the sovereign signifier with a contractual legitimacy of power. It is the wager implicit in the Social Contract that Carlyle places in the centre of *The French Revolution* as a questionable model of reading because its impetus for a "contracted" nationhood is an impetus for the allegorical text. According to Peter France, what Rousseau searches for is the transparent text: "One of Rousseau's central preoccupations was what Jean Starobinski calls 'la transparence,' the desire for direct, uninterrupted communication (or communion) with others, through which he would appear in their consciousness as he knew himself to be. In his own words, 'je voudrais pouvoir en quelque façon rendre mon âme transparente aux yeux du lecteur.'"[11] The wager fulfils the Rousseauian dream of transparency.

This displacement of substance by wager is implied in the opening section of *The French Revolution*, in President Héniault's commentary on the suitability of the King's surname – the "Surname of Bien-Aimé." Carlyle allows Héniault to state the connection between the "interest" the people of Paris showed for their indisposed King and the aptness of that surname as an embodiment of that interest: "At the news of this, Paris, all in terror, seemed a city taken by storm: the churches resounded with supplications and groans; the prayers of priests and people were every moment interrupted by their sobs: and it was from an interest so dear and tender that this Surname of *Bien-Aimé* fashioned itself – a title higher than all the rest which this great Prince has earned" (W, 2:1). As a testimony of word made thing, the passage focuses on a national "interest" that is symbolized by the sovereign's name. Carlyle then proceeds to dismantle this written testimony by inscribing in its wake a completely reversed situation, thirty years later: "Churches resound not with excessive groanings; Paris is stoically calm: sobs interrupt no prayers, for indeed none are offered"; instead of national "interest" in the great Prince's welfare, we have "interest" of another kind – "Priests' litanies, read or chanted at fixed money-rate per hour" – an interest in keeping with the contractual wager of a superannuated Church so popular in Gothic narratives. This sense of a "contracted" interest is further insinuated in the only form of "French Speech" expressed loudly in the streets over the King's final hours – "bets" or wagers made on the time of the King's death. Except for such "contracted" interest, "men ply their useful or useless business as if no Louis lay in danger" (W, 2:2). By exposing Héniault's "interest" to variant readings, Carlyle makes explicit his conception of history as an "infinite Complex of Forces" (W, 3:102), "an infinite conjugation of the verb *To do*," a reality which cannot be comprehended or accounted for by calculation, but which can be perceived as "action and reaction," "All that has been done" contributing to "All that is doing" and "All that will be done" (W, 3:103). Carlyle's conjugation of the verb places his "history" within a nineteenth-century tradition of prophetic reading. According to Aarsleff, the typical prophet is the Victorian sage whose "arsenal is philology," whose "instrument" is etymology. He is the "prophet of words" who insists that words are not merely arbitrary signs but living powers.[12] The sage's preoccupation with the All, the Infinite, is symptomatic of a nineteenth-century concern with linguistic holism, a synecdochic return to a barter economy of mediation.

Perhaps the most illustrative example of this concern is Coleridge's Noetic Pentad, a geometric unfolding of a linguistic economy that anticipates Carlyle's "infinite conjugation." The pentad, like the non-Pythagorean line, illustrates the "relational" basis of all words. While the Pythagorean line is generated by a point *not* contained in the line, that is, an independent point "transcendent to all production," the non-Pythagorean line emerges from a point which, having the extremes of the line as its poles, can be understood as the "indifference of the two poles or correlative opposites" of two extremes. The result is a "point" whose identity is neither fixed nor defined (as matter is). The non-Pythagorean point exercises the fluidity of relational laws; if the poles of the line are termed T (thesis) and A (antithesis), then the I or the mid-point of the line can be "conceived as both [T and A] in as far as it may be either of the two former." I could not be understood as a neutralizing agent in reference to T or A, but would be understood only in its *relative* position to either T or A. Thus "relatively to A, I is equal to T, and relatively to T, it becomes $= A$."[13] The Noetic Pentad, in its declension of the Verb Substantive into five agencies (Prosthesis, Thesis, Antithesis, Mesothesis, Synthesis), similarly places language within a "relational" context. If the idea or meaning of a word is to be neither "an impression on the senses," nor "a definite conception," nor "an abstract notion," it can only be so if it is seen as a "relational" construct, as part of a whole. If the absolutely Real is understood as the "Prosthesis," the subjectively Real as the thesis, and the objectively Real as the "antithesis," then the Idea is the "indifference of the two" (1:219). In the economy of the Noetic Pentad, the logical opposition between irreconcilable differences does not neutralize these differences; each is made "relational," that is, each is made to be the material expression of the other.

In a letter to Josiah Wedgwood, Coleridge emphasizes the "relational" basis between Word and Thing. Arguing against the opposition between Word and Thing produced by Locke's theory of linguistic arbitrariness, Coleridge claims that "Words ... become a sort of Nature to us, & Nature is a sort of Words" because neither Word nor Idea is intelligible when abstracted from its material contingencies, that is, the "all ... with which it had ever been conjoined." Thus "Both Words & Ideas derive their whole significancy from their coherence. The simple *Idea* Red dissevered from all, with which it had ever been conjoined would be as unintelligible as the word *Red*;

the one would be a *sight*, the other a Sound, meaning only themselves, that is in common language, meaning nothing."¹⁴ Word and Thing must participate in a relational economy or "coherence." James C. McKusick in *Coleridge's Philosophy of Language* traces the significance of this "relational" paradigm to Coleridge's theory of language: "Language itself offers a solution to this dilemma [i.e. opposition between Word and Thing] by suggesting that thoughts and things are somehow interchangeable. Subject and object are ultimately reconciled in the mind's ability to 'thingify' – that is, to generate discrete objects by applying linguistic categories to the flux of outward phenomena."¹⁵ Language functions within the economy of the Noetic Pentad; the word cannot merely be an "arbitrary" sign, for it possesses the organicism of an evolving Nature; its inclination to change and dialectical regeneration makes it a living organism – "hence the mind that possesses language is no longer a passive reporting of sense-data, but a free agent in a universe that is itself active"; hence Coleridge's interest in etymology is an attempt to "[vindicate] the role of conscious volition in the evolution of language."¹⁶

It is this principle of change and dialectical regeneration that makes Coleridge's Noetic Pentad a Carlylean motif. In his transmutation of the National Constitution into a reign of terror, Carlyle insists on the use of Gothic reversal to underscore the "allegorical" nature of a "constituted" nationhood. If the Gothic voice is a necessary reversal of the allegory, it is also part of a universal declension of the symbol. Coleridge's Noetic Pentad allows the allegory to be a redeemable participle of the symbol: "The Anathemas are there, and the miraculous Thing is there" (Carlyle, *W*, 2:212); hence the unequivocal responsibility placed on the reader to "purify" his vision by "transmuting" a part into a whole, a participle into infinite conjugation. From this perspective, one might understand *The French Revolution* to be an attempt to evolve symbol from allegory, with the former dimly constellated in the figure of Napoleon who, like the Constitution at the end, finally unifies the country because both, being representations by "acclamation" (*W*, 4:320), are motivated signifiers of French nationhood.

The allegory's resistance to change is identified in *The French Revolution* with a whole repertoire of fixed initiatives. In their attempt to "fix" a declensional phenomenon, such initiatives become formulaic imperatives that Carlyle associates with a money or processional economy. Using the ritual promenade to signify an abstracted and conventionalized hierarchy, Carlyle deliberately dissolves the procession into riot. This procession-turned-riot can be perceived to be the fundamental structure of Carlyle's scenes of reading; implicit in the reversal is a statement on the untenable status of linear, processional discourses. He begins the Gala Procession at Versailles, for example, with an invocation to readers. Focusing on the patriots sitting or crouching at positions of vantage to watch the proceedings, Carlyle addresses these patriots as "friends" who may sit and look "bodily" or "in thought" (W, 2:133). From their "bodily" sight, Carlyle moves proleptically to envision a battery of future events – the September Massacres, retreats from Moscow, Waterloos, the Reign of Terror, and two centuries of struggle before Quackocracy is finally evolved into Democracy. The patriots' "bodily" vision is a necessarily limited one, but Carlyle is able to "explode" this vision by adopting Goethe's technique of double exposure. Juxtaposed to the linear reader of the Gala Procession is the prophetic reader of the text, the "good reader" whom Carlyle bids to take station with him on some "coign of vantage" (W, 2:135). From this bracketed and bracketing position, they are able not only to witness the procession but to subject its progress to dissolution. Thus the solemn procession in which the various classes are marshalled forth "all in prescribed place and costume" (W, 2:134) is broken by proleptic and retroactive digressions. Minister Necker, for example, who "sees all things in Necker," is admonished by Carlyle for being "a theorem that will not hold" (W, 2:135). Necker's allegorical position is dissolved by Carlyle's proleptic interruption; addressing the Baroness de Staël, Necker's daughter, Carlyle warns her of impending suffering, both for her and her father. Such authorial intrusion into the procession becomes a standard Carlylean technique. He insists on punctuating the "Processionals" of allegorical discourse with gaps and reversals.

The same "exploding" technique characterizes Carlyle's prose, which is composed of sentences frequently interrupted by bracketing and fragmenting devices. Like "fuliginous masses," his sentences wind and unwind in strange labyrinthine fashion, the final clauses often serving as puncturing devices to dissolve the meaning and structure forged in the initial clause. Here is a case in point. Focusing on Demoiselle Théroigne in the procession, Carlyle describes her thus: "Brown eloquent Beauty; who, with thy winged words and glances, shalt thrill rough bosoms, whole steel battalions, and persuade an Austrian Kaiser, – pike and helm lie provided for thee in due season; and, alas, also strait-waistcoat and long lodging in the Salpêtrière!" (W, 2:135). The apostrophizing of Théroigne at the beginning of the passage serves to "constitute" her before the reader's eyes. References to her "winged words" and persuasiveness over the Austrian Kaiser create a sense of invulnerability which is supported by the main clause of the passage – "pike and helm lie provided for thee in due season." This impression, however, is reversed by several fragmenting devices that break up the linear momentum of the main clause – the conjunction "and," the interjection "alas," and the adverb "also" – three interrupting devices that dissolve the continuity of the passage. Reference in the final phrase to her incarceration at the Salpêtrière is an example of the proleptic allusions Carlyle uses to puncture the sense of solidity established in the early part of the sentence.

The same invasive technique is used in his depiction of the processional figures. Often invoking a deliberately epic posture in his characters, Carlyle reverses the situation by exposing the gaps within the posture; for example, the epic machinery he adopts becomes a discourse of equivalence which he unmasks in his search for a more genuinely prophetic voice. "Able Editors must give account of such a day" (W, 2:136), he writes; yet his procession is filled with "unable" editors – a Brissot, a Maillard, Marat, the Abbé Sieyes. The latter he focuses on as the *one* clergyman in the procession, a paucity Carlyle emphasizes as sign of the dissolution of a feudal Church. Abbé Sieyes he defines as a fixed idea "with one passion, that of self-conceit." Soaring into the "transcendentalism" Carlyle associates with the epic imperative, Sieyes is the system builder who will "build Constitutions ... skyhigh – which shall all unfortunately fall before he get[s] the scaffolding." Carlyle locates Sieyes's limitation in his "clear assiduous eyes," so transparent they are unable to read the temper of the times. Arrogantly self-serving and two-dimensional, Sieyes in his statement that "Polity is a science I think I have completed" (W, 2:144) reveals the allegorical status of his ambition. Dominated by a reductive economy, Sieyes can never be more than a formula.

The same invasive rhetoric dissolves Robespierre, whose "Advocacy" heritage endears him to "official persons" but prevents him from genuine vision. "An excellent man of business" (W, 2:141), Robespierre can be nothing more than an allegory. Lafayette, "whose name shall be Cromwell-Grandison and fill the world," is also exposed as the "Washington-Formula." "He can become a hero and perfect character," Carlyle muses, "were it but the hero of one idea" (W, 2:145). The French noblesse in full regalia of the old pomp of chivalry is also unmasked as a superannuated language. Carlyle suggests that at one point the regalia served a purpose because these chivalric figures "did actually *lead* the world" towards battle-spoil "where lay the world's best wages then"; but with a new equivalence in wages ("Men" can "hire Drill-Sergeants now at eighteen pence a-day"), these "goldmantled Chivalry Figures" (*W*, 2:146) have become an obsolete idiom.

While these "unable" readers are shown to participate in a self-ingesting economy, Mirabeau is given his due as a prophetic reader. A man who has "swallowed" all formulas, he is the "spokesman of a Nation bent to do the same." A "fiery fuliginous mass which could not be choked or smothered" but would "fill all France with flames" (*W*, 2:141), Mirabeau is the incarnation of Coleridge's logical opposition. Unlike linear readers who cannot go beyond a fixed idea, Mirabeau is able to negotiate a passage between self and community: "in that forty-years' 'struggle against despotism,' he has gained the glorious faculty of *self-help*, and yet not lost the glorious natural gift of *fellowship*, of being helped." "Rare union" (*W*, 2:140) indeed, Mirabeau is the incarnation of the brotherhood of literacy so sorely needed to bring prophetic vision into reality.

Carlyle's reliance on double exposure makes the reading of his Procession an engagement of the prophetic Imaginary. The participants and watchers of the procession on 4 May 1789 could have seen nothing more than a "silent marching mass", yet "[t]he whole Future is there ... in the hearts and unshaped thoughts of these men" (*W*, 2:134). From their "coign of vantage" (*W*, 2:135), author and reader, however, are able to recuperate this experience of the prophetic Imaginary; from their position above and beyond the strictures of linear time, they are able to constitute the "meanest Day" into a "conflux of two Eternities" (*W*, 2:134). The same brotherhood of literacy is "enacted" in a later procession – the funeral procession of Mirabeau. Here, onlookers and processional marchers are made one by a death which is ironically the only event in *The French Revolution* to bring the French people into a genuine brotherhood. Carlyle associates the occasion with the death of Louis XII when public sympathy *was* the material expression of the public's loss: the town criers and the people mourned in unison the death of their sovereign. "King Mirabeau is now the lost King," Carlyle writes, "and one may say with little exaggeration, all the People mourns for him." The National Assembly weeps; the Notables, both patriot and aristocratic, weep; the Sansculottic People, clamorous and resistant on other occasions, listen eagerly to the bourne-stone orators "as men will to any Sermon, or *Sermo*, when it *is* a spoken Word meaning a Thing, and not a Babblement meaning No-thing" (*W*, 3:143). Word and thing unified, orator and listener participate in an economy of "reading" that transcends the partisanship of the times. In the procession of a hundred thousand mourners composed of National Guard, National Assembly, Jacobin society, King's ministers, aristocrats, and patriots, one reads the symbol of nonsectarian fellowship. The brotherhood of grief emerging from the "infinite hum of men" (W, 3:144) as they make their way to the Churchyard Sainte-Catherine becomes a moment of prophetic reading: sign and meaning recuperated in a symbol of communal interest.

The rupture of sign from meaning is the basis of Carlyle's double exposure in *The French Revolution*. Almost every event in *The French Revolution* recreates the double exposure of Goethe's Great Hall Masque: each incident becomes a site of betrayal when the characters involved are "exploded" by a set of "contractual" assumptions. Each incident in *The French Revolution* can be perceived as a scene of misreading that situates the revolutionary impetus within an ironic configuration. The philosophes of pre-revolutionary France, for example, are betrayed by their "paper" idiom. In his association of the philosophes with the Age of Gold, Carlyle makes pre-revolutionary France an age of substitution. The new Age of Gold, Carlyle claims in "Astrea Redux," is the Age of Paper, "which in many ways is the succedaneum of Gold," for it is "Bank paper, wherewith you can still buy when there is no gold left" (W, 2:29). Promoting a theory of perfectibility, the philosophes and a "whole Reformed France" participate in a logic of general reductiveness; paper is substituted for gold. In this paper euphoria, vice loses its deformity and becomes "almost a kind of 'sweet' virtue" (W, 2:30). Happiness reigns supreme, guaranteed almost by "Victorious Analysis" and the "Progress of the Species." Carlyle mocks the easy transparency of philosophism in which "Benevolence" is touted as the "indivisibility" of the state: "if each will, according to rule of Benevolence, have a care for all, then surely – no one will be uncared for" (W, 2:31). Benevolence, happiness, victorious analysis are all parts of what Carlyle sees to be the contractarian ideology of the times – an ideology suggesting that society can be "rightly constituted" by contract and wager: "has not Jean Jacques promulgated his new Evangel of a *Contrat Social*; explaining the whole mystery of Government, and how it is *contracted* and bargained for, – to universal satisfaction?" (W, 2:54). The artificiality of philosophism Carlyle implies through the "grand events" of the age: the masquerade and theatricals which he condemns as "frivolous foam of Existence" (W, 2:32), a champagne foam, waltzing "life-minuet" over "bottomless abysses" (W, 2:25). The leaders of the age have misread the signs of the times. Lumping the working people (all twenty to twenty-five million of them) together into a "kind of dim compendious unity," the "philosophe" government has forgotten that "the masses consist all of units," every unit of whom "has his own heart and sorrows; stands covered there with his own skin, and if you prick him he will bleed" (W, 2:33). So reductive is the King's understanding of his people that when the masses present their petition of grievances at Versailles, the King misreads the "hieroglyphic writing"; he answers by hanging two of the petitioners on a "new gallows forty feet high" (W, 2:34). Carlyle juxtaposes the King's misreading of the masses to Mirabeau's prophetic reading of the same events. Criticizing the King for the "indifference" of his "pen," Mirabeau warns that what the King fancies he can "starve with impunity" will turn into "catastrophe" (W, 2:35).

Pre-revolutionary France, avid in its circulation of paper epigrams, is a "simulacrum" (W, 2:36), like the Montgolfier balloon which simulates, but is not, transcendence. "Windbag" language "scale[s] the Empyrean" with promise and hope only to "*de*mount all the more tragically" (W, 2:51). No less promising is the "fiscal genius" of Controller Calonne, whose connection with "moneyed classes" (W, 2:66) makes him a logical signifier of the age's inflationary culture. Calonne is a "man of incredible facility; facile action, facile elocution, facile thought"; a man by whom "crooked things are become straight" and "rough places plain," he makes his work universally comprehensible – "ready money" (W, 2:67) which he borrows and squanders without restraint. Calonne's mismanagement of the deficit is symptomatic of the nation's proclivity for self-deception. Like the pamphlets and placards with which "ready-writers" (W, 2:94) flooded Paris, Calonne's "paper" measures are allegorical proxies, spectral strategies of appeasement. Unable to move beyond a "moneyed" text, relying only on "promissory conciliatory eloquence" (W, 2:77), Calonne misreads the terms of the wager; anticipating a self-advancing term as prime minister, Calonne is plunged instead into a "recessionary" text when he comes face to face with an unstaunchable deficit. Like *Melmoth the Wanderer*, which is built on an accumulation of unknowns, the financial history of pre-revolutionary France is a Gothic accumulation of deficit.

Calonne's misreading is typical of the times; it is echoed in the "internecine" conflict between his successor Loménie and the People's Parlement of Paris. Described as a "grasping old man" who used his office to further social ambition, Loménie is too immersed in a money economy to make a prophetic reading of the times. The incarnation of a promissory age, he sidesteps economic crisis by issuing "phantom" payments – "three-fifths in Cash and the remaining two-fifths – in Paper bearing interest" (W, 2:109). Unwilling to come to terms with a resistant Parlement, he works to *cauterize* it (W, 2:106). Perceiving the "*fluent* population of Paris" as a "loud destructive Deluge" (W, 2:84), Loménie handles popular dissension by exiling the dissenters to the margin. Thus he circumvents the People's Parlement by establishing minor and plenary courts to handle civil lawsuits. Assuming that the public, "fond of cheap Justice" (*W*, 2:97), will favour these King's Government courts and thus render Parlement inactive, Loménie hatches his anti-Parlement plot "under lock and key" at the King's chateau (*W*, 2:98). When Parlement member D'Esprémenil uncovers the plot, Loménie arrests him and disbands Parlement. For Carlyle, Loménie's "cauteries" (*W*, 2:106) are a misreading of the times. The political body, subjected to scenes of discipline, becomes a "recessionary" text. Resentment against Loménie mushrooms into the Jacobin Society; the Plenary Court, "[a]ssaulted by a universal storm of mingled ridicule and execration," "literally expire[s] at birth" (*W*, 2:105). The cauterized body of the state returns with Gothic vengeance in Carlyle's proleptic narrative: Loménie, forced by mocking Jacobin bailiffs to drink with them from his own wine-cellar and feast with them from his own larder, dies with "three actual cauteries" on his "worn-out body" (*W*, 2:106). Loménie is a Faustian text; his fifty years of effort have become an abortive exchange. "Thou hast got thy robe of office" Carlyle writes, "as Hercules had his Nessus'-shirt" (*W*, 2:107). Despite his presentation of the Loménie-Parlement conflict as a scene of misreading, Carlyle insists on making his narrative a form of corrosive purification. Thus he insists on setting the Loménie allegory next to its prefigured symbol – Napoleon Buonaparte. The "Sham-Priest," caught between a Gothic ambition and a Gothic death, is placed beside a Young Napoleon whose "dusky" complexion anticipates the taciturn earnestness of the later Citizen-King (*W*, 2:107).

Loménie's misreading of the People's Parlement is re-enacted in the débâcle between Broglie and the Third Estate. The latter having "triumphed" into a National Assembly, the Court moves to consolidate its military position. This Court Carlyle describes in epic terms as the "gods of the Oeil-de-Boeuf" who "have withdrawn into the darkness of their cloudy Ida ... shaping and forging what may be needful, be it 'billets of a new National Bank,' munitions of war or things for ever inscrutable to men" (*W*, 2:168). From their abstracted position, the gods misread the temper of the times. They dismiss the possibility of a Parisian revolt; they misread the new political idiom of the people; arrogantly dismissing the Third Estate as a "*canaille* of unwashed Sansculottes*,*" the Court over-calculates the strength of their "moneyed" signifier – Brave Broglie who they feel "'with a whiff of grapeshot ... will give final account of it" (*W*, 2:170). From their epic retreat on a "cloudy Ida," the gods can "see nothing." Why, Carlyle asks, do "Messeignieurs and Broglie the great god of war, on seeing these things ... not pause, and take some other course, any other course?" "They could see nothing," he concludes; dominated by a "moneyed" consciousness, they rush in to "seek their hour"; abstracted from the material text, they are unable to read the signs of an emerging economy: at Béthune, soldiers refuse to disperse a grain riot; the Gardes Françaises, the "best regiment of the line," resist the order to fire; new dragoons called out to replace unwilling militia have, in their turn, drunk with the people "to the King and the Nation, with greatest cordiality" (W, 2:171).

The new political text is ushered in with the dissolution of an old entrenched language of power and the consolidation of this language in universal terms; this idiom of power Carlyle places in the "arms" which, with the sound of the alarm-tocsin resonating in the streets of Paris, become a new logic of general equivalence. Indeed money and weapons emerge in *The French Revolution* as the new idiom of equality. Part of the contractarian mandate of an emerging democracy, arms make not only the man but the nation as well. From Broglie's cannonball to home-made pikes, we witness the transmutation of an old and privileged signifier – "might" – into the universal idiom of "right." Thus Paris explodes with new signifiers of equivalence – arms and the green cockade. The streets are strewn with the dismembered signs of the old order: busts that are hewed asunder, wax busts of Necker and D'Orléans covered with funeral crape, a Garde Française struck dead, his body left beside his shredded uniform (W, 2:175–7). From every window "it *vomits*," this new idiom of equivalence, for "torrents of furniture" and private property are transferred into public hands (W, 2:181). In the same way, an epic machinery made "public" by the carnivalesque emerges in the mock-heroic tone of Carlyle's narration. Superimposing the epic imperative over an equivocal double, Carlyle mounts his war-god "preternatural, with his redhot cannonballs" over a raging subterranean world "from below, a preternatural Brigand-world," menacing with "dirk and fire-brand" (W, 2:179). A ruptured signifier, the epic voice remains an allegorical convention, as spectral as the old Château Mirabeau, "[fading] ... like a shadow on the great still mirror-sea" (W, 2:186) until a new voice (like the prophetic reader's) is able to generate from the din a genuine symbolic economy. Thus Broglie's "whiff of grapeshot" remains at best allegorical, a prefiguring of Napoleon's "sharp and sharpest shot" (W, 4:320) fired six years later to quell remaining insurrectionary sections. The revisionary epic, revived in Napoleon, as classicism is revived in Goethe's Helena, is the brotherhood of the incarnational text.

Almost every event in *The French Revolution*, then, is a site of misreading. The epic machinery of Broglie and Loménie suppresses a prophetic reading of the political scene. Broglie's hubris and Loménie's "facility" are part of an epic discourse Carlyle exposes to be ineffectual before a raging sansculottism. The "hard grapeshot" of Broglie remains a phantom proxy of the "real" thing, serving only to fan a spark to conflagration. If the source of Broglie's misreading is "Pride, which goes before a fall" (W, 2:173), the source of De Launay's misreading in the storming of the Bastille is indecision. This Carlyle makes clear in his opening exploration of the event. De Launay, said to be "profuse of beverages," makes the cowardly decision not to fire, but to be "ruled considerably by circumstances." As Carlyle comments, "Soft speeches will not serve; hard grapeshot is questionable; but hovering between the two is *unquestionable*" (W, 2:190). De Launay's "distraction" results in the Gothic consummation of a superannuated fortress. The "death-agony" of the Bastille is the unfolding of a "historical" pentad: "Jail, Jailoring and Jailor, all three, such as they may have been must finish" (W, 2:195) and assume new and more prophetic forms. The later display of De Launay's "bloody hair-queue, held up in a bloody hand" (W, 2:196–7) makes of the old Marquis De Launay, military warden of the Bastille, a beheaded signifier to be replaced ironically by the guillotine before its genuine symbolic form is manifested by Napoleon's "whiff of grapeshot."

The same misreading dominates the patriots' seizure of the entrance gates, an action Carlyle depicts as an abortive wager. Swiss Guards, who have been defending the Bastille, request the following terms of surrender: "Pardon, immunity to all! Are they accepted?" The terms are all too quickly accepted by the patriots on the "word of an officer" (W, 2:195), the Officer Hulin, who, as soon as entrance is made into the Bastille, abandons the terms of surrender. The Gothicism which ensues comes irrevocably from a deliberate convergence of present and spectral voices, with the present making an ironic commentary on the past. This Carlyle does by depicting history as layers which only a prophetic reader can read in a flash of insight. Thus the Gardes Françaises who stand "unparticipating, with Brennus d'Agoust at the Palais de Justice, when Fate overtook D'Espréménil" have now "participated" in the siege of the Bastille "and will participate ... henceforth" as the "*Centre Grenadiers of the National Guard*" (W, 2:198). The "infinite conjugation" of the Gardes Françaises is reflected as well in the Bastille stones, which will also go through a similar "metamorphosis" into the "Pont Louis Seize" over the Seine waters (W, 2:209). Carlyle insists on superimposing the present over a past so that each becomes an ironic annotation of the other. A case in point can be made of his unearthing of a forgotten letter buried in the Bastille archives: "Read this portion of an old Letter: 'If for my consolation Monseigneur would grant me, for the sake of God and the Most Blessed Trinity, that I could have news of my dear wife, were it only her name on a card, to show that she is alive! It were the greatest consolation I could receive; and I should for ever bless the greatness of Monseigneur'" (W, 2:198–9). The reading of this letter within the context of the siege makes history an "infinite conjugation" within an economy of infinite ironies.

A prophetic reader becomes part of this "infinite conjugation" by allowing the ironies to function as necessity, as necessary "gaps" within the economy of reading. Iser contends that interaction between reader and text can be generated only when the former is willing to overcome the "blanks" within the text by creating paradigms of connectability:

In literature ... the text is structured in such a way that it allows for and, indeed, frequently runs counter to the given disposition of its readers. The blanks break up the connectability of the schemata and thus they marshal selected norms and perspective segments into a fragmented, counterfactual, contrastive or telescoped sequence, nullifying any expectation of *good continuation* ... The greater the number of blanks, the greater will be the number of different images built up by the reader ... We react to an image by building another more comprehensive image.[17]

Carlyle's prophetic reader, therefore, will not misread the text by grasping and measuring this "immeasurable Thing" or "account for it" by reducing it "to a dead logic formula." Unlike linear readers, the prophetic reader will not fear the gap or the thing but "recognize it for what it is, the portentous inevitable end of much, the miraculous beginning of much" (W, 2:213). The prophetic reader becomes part of an infinite economy of ironies.

The excavated letter, like the "skeletons found walled-up, on the *oubliettes*" (W, 2:209) of the Bastille, remains a central Gothic motif; its irony resides in the lapse of time and the cross-currents created by a narration that refuses to be linear. The same irony permeates the expectations of patriotism, "dis-imprisoned" from the sovereign signifier but unconstituted as yet into Nationhood. From the perspective of the street Parisian, the general overturn is fraught with irony: the Bastille has been overturned, the National Assembly consolidated, yet "here with us is famine" (W, 2:248). This disjunction between expectation and reality is the basis of Carlyle's use of a superannuated Catholicism in his Gothic machinery. Associating the revolutionaries' "Doctrine of Fraternity" with Old Catholicism, Carlyle places the brotherhood of Jean Jacques Evangel within the context of obsolete and allegorical systems: "all *isms* that make up Man in France are rushing and roaring in the gulf; and the theorem has become a practice, and whatsoever cannot swim sinks" (*W*, 4:205). The galvanic notions of a dying Catholicism become the central Gothic framework for a superannuated royalty and a formulaic Reign of Terror. Church and constitution are aligned as potential sites of parody, the Republic and Old Catholicism both turning into travesties of the genuine "brotherhood" represented by the Eucharist. Thus the royal repast, established as a sign of communion and patronage for the Regiment de Flandre and the Gardes-du-Corps, military bodyguards remaining at Versailles, becomes a potential scene of rupture. Defining the dinner as "the *ultimate* act of communion" because "men that can have communion in nothing else, can sympathetically eat together, can still rise into some glow of brotherhood over food and wine" (*W*, 2:246), Carlyle makes the royal repast an allegorical sign of community. The men's allegiance to the King reduced to "customary loyal toasts," "pot-valorous speech," (*W*, 2:246), pledges to "the Queen's health" and the "trampling of National Cockades" (*W*, 2:247), the royal repast becomes a "Thyestes Repast" (*W*, 2:248) when Paris patriots, insulted by the trampling of their national symbol, interpret the dinner as sacrilegious "consumption" by an exploitative nobility. The result is the march of the Menadic host to Versailles in petition for bread and the patriotic resolution to exterminate the Regiment de Flandre and the Gardes-du-Corps. Carlyle portrays the deputation of fifteen women marching up the Avenue of Versailles towards the château as a confrontation between word and thing. Faced by the women, the King promises comfort and relief. The women dismiss his comfort as "words only ... which will feed nothing" (*W*, 2:265). In desperation, the Menads "not now in desperation but in mass" penetrate the National Assembly and expose the "public speaking and order of the day" as "words," too abstracted to feed a starving nation. The "communion" of the royal repast is inverted into a Gothic fête noire when the Menads are given "Equal Diet" (*W*, 2:268) at the Senate: "For as Erasmus's Ape mimicked, say with wooden splint, Erasmus shaving, so do these Amazons hold, in mock majesty, some confused parody of National Assembly. They make motions; deliver speeches; pass enactments; productive at least of loud laughter. All galleries and benches are filled; a Strong Dame of the Market is in Mounier's Chair" (*W*, 2:272). These women, invading the seats of the National Assembly and feeding on baskets of loaves, wine and sausages, have made a parody of the royal repast and the constitutional aims of the National Assembly. The patriots' search for a genuine communion of interests, a brotherhood of political equivalence, is exposed in this Menadic inversion to be a travesty of words. "To such length have we got in regenerating France," Carlyle writes, for whom the Menadic host is thing confronting word and exposing word as hollow sham. "What is the use of the Penal Code?" these Menads ask, "the thing we want is Bread" (W, 2:273).

Carlyle's parodic inversion of the dinner is an extension of the theme of brotherhood in *The French Revolution*. The Eucharist as symbol of brotherhood and community is displaced in *The French Revolution* by images of consumption, the kind of obsessive devouring Marion Woodman in *Addiction to Perfection* describes as "the eucharist" gone "demonic." This form of devouring is symptomatic of displaced energy which occurs when the "collective container" for "natural spiritual needs" is perverted or when the "natural propensity for transcendent experience, for ritual, for connection to some energy greater than our own" is distorted and the "real" thing is displaced by its phantom proxy. The result, in Woodman's terms, is "bingeing," a compulsive addiction which occurs when "the natural spiritual hunger" not "fed by the sacred, is trapped in the demonic."[18] The "demonic binge"[19] in *The French Revolution* is the Deficit that can "swallow you" (W, 2:64) and indeed has swallowed the French nation; it is starved Saint-Antoine pouncing on a slain warhorse and devouring it "after the manner of ancient Greek heroes"; it is "Rascality [prowling] discursive[,] seeking what it may devour" (W, 2:269); it is as well the guillotine "devouring its own children" (W, 4:254), creating not a "Reign of Liberty, Equality, Brotherhood" but a brotherhood of "Death" (W, 4:263). Dominated by the unconscious imperative, the demonic devourer lives a self-consuming life; he is the madman who "personifies the unconscious wolf energy that does not know what it wants but consumes everything in a crazed desire to be filled with something."[20] Unable to harness his energy under conscious control, he lives the life of a beast: "like unconscious feeling, it merely reacts like an animal."[21] Living within unredeemed energy, the demonic devourer cannot integrate his conscious and unconscious selves; food, for him, becomes an allegorical language, a cyclic and obsessive substitute which can never satisfy because what the devourer ingests is an abstraction; the demonic Eucharist participates in a money economy when food is ingested not for itself, but for its position as a general equivalent. Integration of the conscious and unconscious selves, unlike such devouring "consumption," is a "communion" of selves.

"Integration," writes Woodman, "requires chewing the primitive material in order to digest it"; that is, integration participates in a barter economy when food ingested becomes symbiotically and materially expressed in the body (as nourishment and strength) of the ingester. Integration follows the passage of the Resurrection myth: "matter dies, crucified by the letter of the law, but after three days, rises again, transformed into spirit."[22] Such is the dialectical course that the "Souper Fraternel" or "Brotherly Supper" (*W*, 4:264) must go through before it becomes a genuine brotherhood. Such is the integration which, in Carlylean terms, is the "swallowing of formulas" in order to generate a new idiom. Such is, as well, the distinction Coleridge maintains between the Eucharist as "mere or arbitrary *memento*" (*Works*, 1:469) and the Eucharist as the "symbol of *all* religion." The former reduces the mystery into an "idol"; the latter is "transubstantiation" (*Works*, 6:317), the word made flesh, ingested, digested, and generated into "a higher third" (*Works*, 1:470).

This distinction between demonic and symbolic Eucharist becomes one of the central Gothic motifs in *The French Revolution*. Here, Carlyle echoes the anti-papist sentiments exploited in most Gothic novels as a point of departure for crimes of repression and vengeance. A dead Catholicism is shown to be "skilfully galvanized," its deathbed contortions taking the form of the fire processional or "Auto-da-fé" of Saint-Huruge. A mock puppet of the Pope in plush and tiara and a mock construction of his keys are burnt in effigy with the "enemies" of the people; the "holocaust is consummated" (*W*, 3:155) in the Palais-Royal as a sign of terror to royalty, who sees it, "but says nothing" (*W*, 3:156). Everywhere, dissident priests expelled by constitutional priests solicit a peculiar form of death – "of martyrdom without sincerity, with only cant and contumacy" (*W*, 3:150–1). A dead Catholic Church "not allowed to lie dead" "is *galvanized* into the detestablest death-life" (*W*, 3:151) or paper idiom of allegory.

This Gothic use of a galvanized Catholicism is deployed most fully in Carlyle's presentation of the Carmagnole as demonic Eucharist. Launched by the revolutionary army, the Carmagnole tears down the culture of the Church and substitutes in its place the language of violence or the "armed" word: "One sees them drawn up in marketplaces; travel-splashed, rough-bearded, in *carmagnole complète*; the first exploit is to prostrate what Royal or Ecclesiastical monument, crucifix or the like, there may be: to plant a cannon at the steeple; fetch down the bell without climbing for it, bell and belfry together" (*W*, 4:230). Transmuting the Church into a new logic of equivalence, the revolutionary army melts belfries into cannon, pewter into bullets, mass-books into cartridge-papers. The Carmagnole is presented as a danse macabre (reminiscent of Goethe's "Walpurgis' Night" in *Faust I*) and a parodic Eucharist when the participants are described as being drunk from "the brandy they had swallowed out of chalices" and "eating mackerel on the patenas." Mounted on asses dressed with priests' stoles, in sacrilegious parody of the Eucharist, the participants "held clutched with the same hand communion-cup and sacred wafer" (*W*, 4:226). A further displacement of the Eucharist can be seen in the so-called "Feasts of Reason" described by Carlyle as the "communion service of the New Religion of Chaumette" (*W*, 4:228). Reason, hailed as the new god-term, becomes the exchange value presiding over feasts one can hardly call reasonable: choir loft filled with wine and sausages; children invited to drink from bottles until their "prompt intoxication created laughter"; Reason, dressed in azure mantle, made to sit aloft while cannoneers serve as her acolytes and "mad multitudes," spread around the bonfire of chapel-balustrades, dance the Carmagnole, the "dancers nigh bare of breeches, neck and breast naked" (*W*, 4:228). Carlyle's depiction of the Carmagnole is a mock inversion of the communion of selves.

If this communion of selves is to be a viable and living sign of community, it must be open to renewal. It must extend its tolerance for discrepancies; the expansion of its representative boundary to include as yet unrepresented factions makes this particular brotherhood an ever-expanding circle of "ingestion." Unlike the consumed product which leaves no residue, the communion of selves is always a dialectical accommodation of residual elements. In *A Grammar of Motives*, Kenneth Burke refers to the communion service of pre-industrial Christian tradition as the "focus of public enactment" most valid in its form of "representativeness." That is, the communion service is "synecdochically" representative of the community; like tribal festivals, it is "a moment of convergence ... felt by *all* of the participants to have an integral bearing upon the welfare of the tribe."[23] If communion seeks the many in one, the whole in the part, it is a form of "ingestion" which "swallows formulas" to create a new circumference of identity. Unlike "consumption," which produces nothing, "communion" necessitates a shift in the defining boundaries of wholeness. Communion is a brotherhood of residual being only if the residual being is made to redefine the circumference of the central. A communion of selves can never be a permanent or fixed entity; by its nature as a point of "convergence" among disparate elements, communion seeks to "incorporate" into the body of the community that which was not represented before. It is this aspect which makes communion an act of transformation, for there is a very real sense that the redefined community is a newly generated matrix of tolerance. In this sense as well, communion is not a matter of reform. The reforming agent "gives up his sins and returns to the traditional norms of action"; the transforming agent is "a change in substance or principle, a qualitative shift in the nature of motivation" (357). If the Constitution is to be more than a paper machinery for reform, it has to get beyond mere galvanic measures; it has to change the fundamental nature of motivation itself.

For Burke, such a change is the pivotal distinction between "Motion" and "Act." "A billiard ball," he maintains, "is neither moral nor immoral" for "it cannot act[;] it can only move, or be moved" (136). Motion, therefore, is movement or motive without will; an act is *"causa sui"* or "a motive of itself" (66), independent of extrinsic factors. Motion is promissory in context; its dependence on an external term for validation makes it a transitive factor. An Act is intrinsically motivated, symbolic in focus, for the Act becomes itself a convergence of the container and the contained, the actor and the action. The Constitution conceived as a "motive of itself" internalizes the symbolic dimension of an act of communion. The Constitution conceived as motion is a scene of misreading, its promissory exigencies producing an investment economy which Burke suggests is too binding: "A Constitution is 'binding' upon the future in the sense that it has centred attention upon one calculus of motivation rather than some other; and by thus encouraging men to evaluate their public acts in the chosen terms, it serves in varying degrees to keep them from evaluating such acts in other terms" (368). Promissory allegiances are problematic because "one cannot 'guaranty' a people any rights which future conditions themselves make impracticable" (367). A Constitution which promises the future in the present cultivates an idiom of indebtedness: one holds the future indebted by one's deposit; one makes a connection between the now and the hereafter which validates one's present action. In a Constitution perceived as an act, the hereafter need not validate the present because the present is a motive of itself.

This distinction between act and motion lies at the basis of Carlyle's analysis of the Constitution in *The French Revolution*. As a site of "public enactment," the Constitution must steer its course between motion and act, consumption and communion. Carlyle's presentation of the Feast of Pikes places the constitutional aim within a set of reductive and promissory agencies. He presents the wager as the pivotal ambition of the feast and the pivotal reason for the dissolution of the "fraternity" sworn in by what he calls a "scenic Nation" (*W*, 3:48). This "business of Covenanting," he writes, "is natural to any agitated Nation." In its search for security, the French nation seeks to ratify its nationhood through a "Solemn League and Covenant" (W, 3:42), investing in the act of swearing a promissory machinery. Placing the nation's fervour for the covenant within a "theatrical" medium, Carlyle suggests that the national oath, so solemnly and dramatically enacted at the Feast of Pikes, is unfortunately mainly motion. "Pardonable are human theatricalities," he writes, for they emanate from a "head which with insincerity *babbles*, – having gone distracted." The "Thespian Art" (W, 3:49) of the Feast of Pikes is part of an allegorical idiom, and this Carlyle emphasizes in his presentation of the event as masque. Indeed, both event and preparation for the event are presented as performances: patriot artists busy hollowing out a national amphitheatre; patriot men and women volunteering their services, delving and hewing the Field of Mars (where the amphitheatre is built) as "Adam himself delved." The precipitate involvement of the nation is given in terms reminiscent of a masque processional; each group of patriots is described as the personification of a specific class and the whole processional is staged as an allegory of brotherhood. "Long-frocked tonsured Monks, with short-skirted Water-carriers, with swallow-tailed well-frizzled *Incroyables* of a Patriot turn; dark Charcoalmen, meal-white Peruke-makers; or Peruke-wearers, for Advocate and Judge are there, and all Heads of Districts: sober Nuns sisterlike with flaunting Nymphs of the Opera, and females in common circumstances named unfortunate; the patriot Ragpicker, and perfumed dweller in palaces; for Patriotism, like New-birth, and also like Death, levels all" (W, 3:57). Carlyle infuses the processional with a "plastic" feeling of community and bonding. Personified abstractions, the groups of patriot workers are depicted as pure "noble sentiment" untested by time: "beautiful ... noble sentiment: like gossamer gauze, beautiful and cheap; which will stand no tear and wear" (W, 3:59).

The entire Feast of Pikes itself is similarly presented as a masque performance. The theatricality of the event is emphasized by Carlyle's inclusion of a decision a "misguided Municipality" makes when it suggests that patriots be admitted to the feast by "tickets." Moreover, Carlyle insists on depicting the patriots in attendance as an audience "decked and glorified," waiting for the curtains to be drawn. The entire event is framed as a "picture," the amphitheatre specifically as a "little circular enamel picture in the centre of ... a vase – of emerald." Carlyle deliberately uses an enclosing technique to telescope the event into a scenic tableau; the horizon of curious patriots encircling Paris becomes "one more or less peopled Amphitheatre." All around this central stage stand rings of consuming federates: "on remotest steeple and invisible village belfry stand men with spy-glasses. On the heights of Chaillot are many-coloured undulating groups" (*W*, 3:62). The entire scene is enacted with "spy-glass" vision: all France is reduced to "one Amphitheatre" and all patriots "covenanted" by "firing and swearing." The same telescoping imperative is demonstrated in the Patriots' insistence that the covenant be validated by "sound," as if the *spoken* oath is the only form of guarantee to an agitated nation. The National Assembly must swear; the King must swear "audibly," and the citizens must swear, their oath emanating like the sound of tocsin "to the four corners of France" (*W*, 3:63). In a mock enactment of the Pentecostal descent of tongues, Carlyle exposes the discrepancy between the miraculous and the galvanic: "By what thrice-driven Franklin thunder-rod shall miraculous fire be drawn out of Heaven; and descend gently, lifegiving, with health to the souls of men? Alas, by the simplest: by Two Hundred shaven-crowned Individuals, 'in snow-white albs, with tricolor girdles,' arranged on the steps of Fatherland's Altar; and, at their head for spokesman, Soul's-Overseer Talleyrand-Perigord! These shall act as miraculous thunder-rod, – to such length as they can" (*W*, 3:64). Talleyrand and two hundred pieces of white calico become part of a theatrical machinery that simulates motion. Turning Talleyrand's miracle into a Gothic travesty, Carlyle continues: "while Episcopus Talleyrand, long-stoled, with mitre and tricolor belt, was yet but hitching up the Altar-steps to do his miracle, the material Heaven grew black; a north-wind, moaning cold moisture, began to sing; and there descended a very deluge of rain" (*W*, 3:65). To this end the allegorical idiom must come. From the jousting on the river to the patriotic toasts and universal ball, the reader gets the impression of a "Walpurgis' Night" aptly allegorized on a rescripted Bastille:

Or out, on Earth's breast itself, behold the Ruins of the Bastille. All lamplit, allegorically decorated; a Tree of Liberty sixty feet high; and Phrygian cap on it, of size enormous, under which King Arthur and his round-table might have dined! In the depths of the background is a single lugubrious lamp, rendering dim-visible one of your iron cages, half-buried, and some Prison stones, – Tyranny vanishing downwards, all gone but the skirt: the rest wholly lamp-festoons, trees real or of pasteboard; in the similitude of a fairy grove; with this inscription, readable to runner: *"Ici l'on danse*, Dancing Here." (*W*, 3:66)

The Constitution and its federative work reduced to an allegorical "similitude," it is no wonder that this marriage feast between royalty and the French nation ends not in a communion of selves but in the "blackest" "Consummation of Sansculottism" (W, 4:222). The titles of the chapters on the Feast of Pikes emphasize the allegorical status of this "public enactment." The Feast of Pikes is full of "SOUND AND SMOKE" (W, 3:61); "AS IN THE AGE OF GOLD" (W, 3:55), it simulates, but is not, the symbol.

If the Feast of Pikes shows France "federated" under a national oath, the affair at Nanci is an ironic commentary on this oath. What transpires at Nanci is not so much the triumph of royalty over a mutinous French army as the *"wrong-side* of the thrice-glorious Feast of Pikes, the right-side of which formed a spectacle for the very gods" (W, 3:100). Nanci is the Gothic inversion of the Feast of Pikes; it exposes the national swearing of brotherhood to be only "words" when the same Field of Mars becomes the site for the funeral service of three thousand French soldiers massacred by an epic Bouillé. Bouillé's fixed initiative – to *"quench* [the] conflagration" (W, 3:98) – is portrayed as a source of misreading. He claims that he was "urged by subsequent contradiction" (the possibility of civil war) and "public military rule of duty" to extinguish this contradiction (W, 3:97). He acted, he claims, to prevent national disaster. It is here that Carlyle faults Bouillé for his "epic" vision – the reduction of the event to a Manichean opposition: order against chaos. Such a dualistic vision of the situation refuses to see the order implicit in chaos: "Civil war, indeed, is Chaos; and in all vital Chaos there is new Order shaping itself free: but what a faith this, that of all new Orders out of Chaos and Possibility of Man and his Universe, Louis Sixteenth and Two-Chamber Monarchy were precisely the one that would shape itself" (W, 3:97). Bouillé at Nanci stands as a "real opposition," in which opposing forces are neutralized in a dualistic, mutually exclusive scheme. Thus the confrontation between the officers and the national guards is described as a volcanic encounter between two "tumultuous inflammable masses," "this of keen nitrous oxide, that of sulphurous firedamp" (W, 3:95); the explosion which ensues generates a "bloody" peace which "might have come bloodless" (W, 3:97) had Bouillé made a prophetic reading of the event.

One irony clearly emerges from the affair at Nanci: the constitutional oath and its fraternal principle are translated by the French army into the logic of general equivalence. Carlyle locates the unrest of the regiments in two grievances – the aristocrat officers and peculation of pay (W, 3:74). The universal "right" of man is translated into the "armed" word when Bouillé, encountering the Regiment of Salm, hears their voiced opposition: "Bouillé walks trustfully towards the Regiment de Salm, speaks trustful words; but here again is answered by the cry of forty-four thousand livres odd sous. A cry waxing more and more vociferous, as Salm's humour mounts; which cry, as it will produce no cash or promise of cash, ends in the wide simultaneous whirr of shouldered muskets, and a determined quick-time march on the part of Salm – towards its Colonel's house, in the next street, there to seize the colours and military chest" (W, 3:80–1). Like the "tocsin," which resonates revolutionary clamour, the "armed" word becomes the universally equivalent term, and the miracle which motivates a disciplined army is replaced by the galvanic "democracy" of a military mob.

Carlyle's criticism of the Constitution is further seen when he makes "nationhood" part of a universal mania for equivalence or "Clubbism." The Mother-Society or Jacobin Club, sprouting at first as the "promised feast" (W, 3:31), becomes a "Feast of Lapithae" (W, 3:32) marked by division and bloodshed. In a later passage, Clubbism becomes "the blackbrowed Marseillese" (W, 3:299) marching in unison against the "tyrant of the Chateau" (W, 3:303). Carlyle mockingly refers to this populist spirit in terms of the Romantic lyre: "[a]re not mankind, in whole, like tuned strings, and a cunning infinite concordance and unity; you smite one string, and all strings will begin sounding, – in soft sphere-melody, in deafening screech of madness" (W, 3:299). The Romantic "sphere-melody" ironically transmuted into a "deafening screech of madness" is a statement on the (im)possibility of universal fellowship. A "Representative Government" is an oxymoron at best – "Are Representative Governments mostly at bottom Tyrannies too?" (W, 2:216). Representative government, prolific in "the art of producing zero" (W, 2:217), is part of an abstracted economy. Its reliance on an abstracted term for its validation can be seen in the constitutional definition of the "active" citizen as one who has paid the "marc d'argent" or "yearly tax equal to three-days' labour." For those who cannot or will not participate in this logic, "not the slightest vote for him" even if he has been "*acting*, all year round, with sledge-hammer, with forest-levelling axe" (W, 3:26). By the same token, patriotism is defined through a "cash nexus" policy or "Don Patriotique," a gift of jewels and money donated as sign of one's patriotism; where such donations cannot be obtained with goodwill, the plebian "Court of *Cassation*," by which private properties are rendered "national," invests the act of plunder with patriotic significance (W, 3:118). The "smell ... of cash" (W, 2:240) taken as a sign of allegiance, the Constitution becomes a "minted" nationhood reminiscent of the "gilt assignats" of "The Diamond Necklace." Carlyle emphasizes the reductive and untenable status of the Constitution in his particular notation of the Camp of Jalès, a royalist military camp which existed "mostly on paper." Unable to keep the soldiers (composed mostly of sansculottic peasants and national guards) at Jalès, the royalist captain kept up a fabricated report of the camp "for a terror and a sign – if peradventure France might be re-conquered by theatrical machinery, by the *picture* of a Royalist Army done to the life!" (*W*, 3:11). Like the paper Jalès, the Constitution remains an empty signifier.

The Constitution as a scene of misreading is perhaps best illustrated in Carlyle's treatment of two patriot "headsmen" – Jourdan Coupe-tête in Avignon and Able Editor Marat in Paris. Invested with an equivalent term, the "blue National uniform" of the patriots, Jourdan the Headsman massacres a hundred and thirty aristocrats (men, women, and children) in the isolated castle at Avignon. Carlyle's description of these "Brigand" executions prefigures the guillotine of the September Massacres. Fixed in imperative, Jourdan Coup-Tête is the logical extension of a contractarian ideology of equivalence. In essence, he anticipates Marat. "A Distraction," emblematic of "this distracted Eighteenth Century" (*W*, 2:236), Marat is likewise the paper idiom whose "idea could not become an action, but only a fixed-idea" (*W*, 4:24). Keeper of the Committee of Watchfulness (Surveillance), Marat dissolves opposition through the guillotine. In his panopticon earnestness, Marat becomes the apotheosis of suspicion, the linear eye of death which Carlyle juxtaposes to the phantasmagoric eye of history. In Marat, we see the Gothic inversion of a "Realized Idea" (*W*, 4:9) when the one and indivisible republic is turned into a republic of death. His literal vision becomes the citizen's "armed" word – the guillotine serving a most macabre form of "Public Salvation" by dispensing equality through execution, the guillotine becoming a macabre form of "minting" by "coining money on the Place de la Révolution": "For always, the 'property of the guilty' ... is confiscated" (*W*, 4:213); the "Law of Forty Sous" guarantees Jacobin life by paying citizens to attend the society's bi-weekly meetings; the "Law of the Suspect" erases all opposition by turning residual or contrary populations into prey; the "Law of the Maximum" forces the farmers to sell, even at a loss, by "fixing the highest price of grains" (*W*, 4:142). Everywhere, Church and private properties are "minted" into a new idiom of "right": church bells "melted down into the furnace to make cannon"; the church railings torn up and "hammered into pikes"; the coffins of the churchyard melted "into balls" (*W*, 4:11); Paris cellars excavated for saltpetre, an essential ingredient for the production of gunpowder; in all places, arms and "*Pro patria mori*" (*W*, 4:236) become the new banners of equivalence. With grim irony, Carlyle turns Marat's Committee of Public Surveillance into a macabre language of death. This is most evident in his transcription of Peltier's Paris during the September Massacres:

From five in the afternoon, a great city is struck suddenly silent; except for the beating of drums, for the tramp of marching feet; and ever and anon the dread thunder of the knocker at some door, a Tricolor Commissioner with his blue Guards (*black*-guards!) arriving. All streets are vacant, says Peltier; beset by Guards at each end: all Citizens are ordered to be within doors. On the River float sentinel barges, lest we escape by water: the Barriers hermetically closed. Frightful! The Sun shines; serenely westering, in smokeless mackerel-sky; Paris is as if sleeping, as if dead: – Paris is holding its breath, to see what stroke will fall on it ... polished satire changed now into coarse pike-points (hammered out of railing); all logic reduced to this one primitive thesis, An eye for an eye, a tooth for a tooth!   (W, 4:14–15)

Abstracted from material existence, the constitutional wager is transmuted into a language of vengeance: polished satires are sharpened into pike points, tricolor national guards become black-guards. Paris is hermetically sealed with a reductive logic. The sun shines, but with Gothic irony. The conversion of mob culture into a sterile language of equivalence is made all the more grim by the details Carlyle includes in the passage: the vacant streets, the citizens ordered to be within doors; the silent city. The contractarian ideology, for all its popular appeal, is exposed as a treacherous and abortive wager.

For Carlyle, the Reign of Terror is a necessary inversion of the Feast of Pikes. Almost every atrocity he mentions is seen in the context of an earlier, more ideal and eucharistic vision. Communal bonding, for example, is travestied in the so-called "Republican Marriage," by which dissenting couples are "tied together, feet and feet, hands and hands," and drowned in the sea (W, 4:222). The National Carroccio, "car-borne" (W, 2:151), becomes the death tumbril or revolution cart, carting away the corpses to be stripped of clothes, skin, and hair before their burial in inconsequential graves. Thus Carlyle makes provocative mention of the blond perukes "made from the Heads of Guillotined women" and the "perfectly good wash-leather" made from the skins of guillotined men at the Mendon tannery. With facetious irony, Carlyle turns the perverse into a logic of equivalence: "The locks of a Duchess, in this way, may come to cover the scalp of a Cordwainer" (W, 4:246–7). Despite these atrocities, Carlyle sees the Reign of Terror as a step in the evolution of the symbol. In book 5, he claims that the "horrors of the French Revolution" were properly the "*shadow*" of the phenomenon, the "negative part of it" (W, 4:203), the phenomenon being the Thing which "came not to range itself under old recorded Laws of Nature at all, but to disclose new ones." The problem for Carlyle is finding a way to read this Thing correctly, to name it, for "were the right Name itself once here, the Thing is known henceforth; the Thing is then ours, and can be dealt with" (W, 4:204). To read prophetically is the quest in *The French Revolution* and this prophetic reading demands that we see Nature's laws as infinite; the Thing becomes a dialectical assimilation of the old into the new, for "Despair, pushed far enough, completes the circle ... and becomes a kind of genuine productive hope again" (W, 4:205).

It is this "genuine productive hope" that forms the basis of Carlyle's response to Edmund Burke's *Reflections on the Revolution of France*. Burke's despair is generated by his determination to see the French revolutionary government as a "philosophic" purchase, an appropriation of sign over substance such that the indelible "primeval contract ... sanctioned by the inviolate oath which holds all physical and all moral natures, each in their appointed place" is broken by a "theoretic experimental edifice."[24] While Burke's critique of the allegory is diametrically opposed to the Burkean dream of substance, Carlyle's allegory is part of a prophetic "phantasmagory" in which the allegory, if read in the right spirit, can be made into a type or prefigurement of the symbol. Burke's "shop of horrors"[25] can be accommodated within a vision of dialectical regeneration so that the economics of terror can become the economy of the event. Carlyle emphasizes this dialectical reading of the event in his critique of the emigrant nobles in book 5. Spurred by Burke's *Reflections on the Revolution in France*, these nobles "acted fatally on France" by misreading the sansculottic insurrection as a "flaw" to be righted by the sovereign signifier. They read in the burning of the château the displacement of substance by a "blustering Effervescence"; "had they understood their place and what to do in it," Carlyle continues, "this French Revolution, which went forth explosively in years and in months, might have spread itself over generations; and not a torture-death but a quiet euthanasia have been provided for many things" (W, 3:232–3). It is the aristocracy's inability to understand their own allegorical position that contributes to the "violence" of the revolution; had they understood their position in the economy of the event, they too could have been prophetic readers of a historical Imaginary; they too could have perceived the rupture of the sign as a necessarily synecdochic "materialism of the incorporeal."[26]

Carlyle's insistence on the economy of the event as an inevitable evolution of violence can be seen in his juxtaposition of the Gironde-Mountain conflict to the Girondin-Jacobin conflict. Carefully distinguishing between a Girondin formula for a respectable "Republic for the Middle Class" (*W*, 4:115) and a Mountain impetus for the genuine and the miraculous, Carlyle invests this conflict with the economy of the event: this battle of the Mountain and Girondins is the battle of "Fanaticisms and Miracles" (*W*, 4:120); it is the rupture of the signifier from the signified, rendering "all Laws that are not Laws of Nature ... naught and Formulas merely" (*W*, 4:116). Like the Blakean metaphor of "printing in the infernal method, by corrosives ... melting apparent surfaces away and displaying the infinite which was hid,"[27] Carlyle's Gironde-Mountain conflict attests to the infinity of prophetic vision. As a site of misreading, the Girondin formula over-subscribes to a "Moneybag of Mammon" culture. Perceiving money to be the "symbol" of what "the respectable Republic for the Middle Classes will signify," the Girondins have subscribed to the "worst and basest of all banners and symbols of dominion among men." The infinity within the sansculottic vision is its search for validity "not in the Money-bag, but far elsewhere" (*W*, 4:115). Confrontation between Girondins and Mountain, therefore, can generate the symbol.

Not so, however, the Girondin-Jacobin conflict, which is narrated in the incident of the sale of sugar. The sale of sugar five weeks after the beheading of the King is subjected to a battery of misreading by both Girondins and Jacobins. The Girondins perceive the sale to be "pregnant indications" of a Pitt plot. The Jacobins' misreading of the sale is equally virulent. In reconstructing both Girondin and Jacobin formulas to explain the sale of sugar, Carlyle reproduces the "fixed" intensity of a conflict bound to neutralize itself out of existence. Unlike the Gironde-Mountain conflict, which takes on the dimension of Coleridge's "logical opposition" because it generates the dim outline of the symbol, the Girondin-Jacobin conflict is mutually exclusive. Girondin and Jacobin formulas are fabricated on the "Faust" plot: someone has "sold out" and what was a "concrete Phenomenon to the eye" (*W*, 4:117) transpires as theoretic suspicion. What these factions fail to see Carlyle shares with his reader in a fraternal act of communion. "Yes, Reader," he writes, "here is the miracle" – the faith "flaming in the heart of a People" for a "Fraternal Heaven-on-Earth" (*W*, 4:119). What the reader is asked to see is not only the deception implied in a "thrice-glorious Feast of Pikes" (*W*, 3:100), but the idea that despite the "hubbub of voices in distraction" and the "shrieks of despair" (*W*, 4:120), one can genuinely find the "Faith undoubtedly of the more prodigious sort" (*W*, 4:119) working itself out of the tumult and the violence. It is here that Carlyle extends his "genuine productive hope" into a genuine brotherhood of literacy.

"To the eye of equal brotherly pity," he writes, "innumerable perversions dissipate themselves; exaggerations and execrations fall off, of their own accord. Standing wistfully on the safe shore, we will look, and see, what is of interest to us, what is adapted to us" (W, 4:120). This "eye of equal brotherly pity" will neither fear nor castigate the "exaggerations and execrations," but will purify from the dross "what is of interest to us, what is adapted to us"; the prophetic readers will not dismiss the confusion, but will work to purify the symbol from the allegory. The prophetic readers will not so glibly dismiss the Revolution as a "shop of horrors." They will, however, stand wistfully on the shore; witnessing the transaction of the whole, they become a "supplement" to the text, an off-shore commentary that can find some means of reunifying a ruptured bond.

The reader as "supplement" is the basis of an embedded text in the chapter entitled "September in Argonne." An embedded text participates as supplement; it facilitates a barter economy of reading by allowing what might easily have been overlooked to constellate meaning for those willing to see in the decapitated signifier the economy of the event. In this particular case, the text is a description of cannon-fever made by "World-Poet" Goethe. Embedded in the conflict between the Prussian Duke of Brunswick and Patriot Dumouriez, the fragment becomes a means by which Carlyle wrests from chaos the sign of an emerging symbol: "in this shrieking Confusion, and not elsewhere, lies the first germ of returning Order for France" (W, 4:54). Goethe's excerpt stands as testimony of the "scientific desire to understand what that same cannon-fever may be" (W, 4:55), as a genuine scene of prophetic reading. The world-poet enters the "dance and firing of the cannon-balls," despite warnings otherwise, to "understand" cannon-fever through the adoption of "similitude," through participation in a conditional "as if" world in order to rescue from it the unconditional truth. "By degrees you get a very uncommon sensation; which can only be described by similitude. It seems as if you were in some place extremely hot, and at the same time were completely penetrated by the heat of it; so that you feel as if you and this element you are in were perfectly on a par. The eye-sight loses nothing of its strength or distinctness; and yet it is as if all things had got a kind of brown-red colour, which makes the situation and the objects still more impressive on you" (W, 4:55). Unlike most who would have run from the scene in terror, Goethe makes of the terror a "Death-Birth," a site of prophetic encounter. Carlyle makes him an emblem of the French Revolution: "In [his] irrecognizable head, meanwhile, there verily is the spiritual counterpart (and call it complement) of this same huge

Death-Birth of the World." Goethe's "infinity" lies in his refusal to let confusion be and his determination to work its allegorical idiom into the economy of the symbol. Both Goethe and Carlyle stand together, part of a brotherhood of literacy which can redeem from what is well-nigh "irrecognizable" the rudiments of "scientific historic fact" (W, 4:55). Together they vindicate the place of the reader in a hermeneutical tradition that is moving away from exegesis to psychology.[28] In this sense, the reader can probably be perceived as the "hero" of *The French Revolution*; he can be seen as an extension of Mark Cumming's "hero" – the "symbol maker, the shaper of 'Realised Ideals' by which to live."[29]

4 Economics and Economy in the King's Glorious Body

The distinction Carlyle maintains between allegory and symbol is a significant feature of the royal icon. Royal portraits present a unique relationship between body and sign, between the historical body of the King and his portrait, the "constituted" sign of royal power. That which is hidden by these portraits reveals their participation in what de Man calls "metaphorical totalization,"[1] strategies through which an icon suppresses historical reality in its unilateral pursuit of ideal presentation. In *Allegories of Reading: Figural Language in Rousseau, Nietzsche, Rilke and Proust*, de Man dissolves Rousseau's *Social Contract* by showing that it is a text divided against itself, a position Carlyle sustains as well in *The French Revolution* by subjecting the royal sign of French kingship to "bodily" dissolution. In this chapter, I will argue that this relationship between body and sign is enacted in *The French Revolution* as the body's rupture, a rupture which can also be seen as evidence of Carlyle's ambivalence towards his own ailing body. The "convalescent" mentality of which he was so fond is more than reflection of a bilious personality; it becomes, indeed, the point at which body and text intersect as sites of disclosure.

During the course of his reign, Louis XIV commissioned Hyacinth Rigaud to complete a portrait of him as the royal monarch. According to Louis Marin in *Food for Thought*, this portrait becomes the iconic sign of the King's "Glorious Body," incarnated as the political body of the people; thus the portrait of King Louis XIV reverberates beyond the historical Louis XIV to embody a political community: "The process whereby the image is reflected back upon itself is perhaps what makes the portrait both an iconic equivalent of the proper name, an autonym ... [and] a form of epideixis, that is, of a positive demonstration, of a unique exemplification, or presentational intensification: 'I am the King' or better still, '*L'État, c'est moi.*'"[2] The royal portrait inhabits a double discourse, what Marin calls a "conjunction of the King's two bodies ... the unchanging and eternal body of dignity and ... the individual body that is subject to all the miseries and sufferings of nature" (219). In the former, we see an iconography that is purposefully enhanced so that the portrait impresses the spectator as a "miraculous or marvelous gesture" (220). Because the natural and individual body is sacrificed to the "miraculous" gesture of the iconic body, the royal portrait remains, in Marin's words, a "fetish" rather than a representation. The royal portrait is an indication of a royal obsession with power: "Tyranny, the desire for absolute power, for all power, is a desire for death, and the portrait of the King is a figure of its realization in the fetish of representation" (208). The royal portrait therefore fails to be the Eucharistic symbol. It is the substitute for the King; it is *not* the King.

But how can a portrait become the King? For Marin, this "transubstantiation" is possible only when the portrait affirms the presence of the King's dual bodies. The economy of the symbol resides in what Marin perceives to be a double split "in the identity of the thing." The first time, this identity "divides into a thing and a sign; the second time, the nature of the sign requires a distinction between the thing that does the representing and the thing that is supposed to remain what it is." In the economy of the symbol, thing is not sacrificed to meaning. Like Coleridge, Marin insists that the sign partake of that which it enunciates. It is this participation that gives Marin's sign the dimensions of a "logical opposition." The sign's participation as thing creates an "aporia," "constituted by an absolute difference within an absolutely maintained identity"; this aporia "can only be overcome by modeling the structure of the sign-representation on that of a secret: something is hidden, but not totally, for then the secret would disappear." While a fetish erases the secret, the symbol flourishes in its trace; "[i]t is crucial that the secret secretes it presence" because "the secret's secretion constitutes the reality of its presence" (11). The King's portrait becomes the King's body only when the historical body is affirmed with and by the miraculous one.

This distinction between a representation effecting a "remainderless exchange" (219) between thing and sign and a representation whose exchange is circumscribed within its "absolute difference" or aporia is central to Marin's typography of the royal sign. To this end, Marin performs two different readings on the two different forms of exchange established within the tradition of royal portraits and medals. His first reading focuses on the royal portrait and historical medals (and coins) celebrating the King's idealized power. An allegorical representation, concludes Marin, is a "remainderless exchange between the historical body [of the King] and the body politic [of the people]" (220). The historical medal, like the sovereign coin, and the royal portrait accomplish this operation by erasing all traces of the King's private and natural body in the icon. Thus "legible and visible on the two sides are the name and effigy of the King, his deeds and perfection, all brought together in a single place and time. A sovereign body coined as a monarchial and a theologico-political host, such a medal has no hidden side. Rather, the absolute reveals and signifies itself in the monumental truth of its dazzling glory" (220). This medal or sovereign coin effects a "remainderless" reconciliation such that the coin becomes a "perfect host, one sacrificed to the omniscience of the Monarch by virtue of historiography and iconography." Thus, this medal or coin effects the totalitarian brotherhood Carlyle portrays in the Thyestes repast of *The French Revolution*. Marin betrays the dangers of such iconographic representation when he states that "the medal transforms the individuals who have been graciously invited to attend the King's banquet into subjects *subjected* to his sovereign power" (220, italics mine).

This subjection or subjugation is made possible by the agglomeration of royal insignia in both portrait and medal. Making an intense scrutiny of Rigaud's royal portrait, Marin notes that every single element in the painting is a "symbolic ornament or a piece of history" (200), everything from the gold canopy and crimson carpet in the background to the ritual wig worn by the monarch. Every item in the royal portrait both decorates and points to the royal body in its role as "a suppositum for these treasures." The body is given reality and "made present" through an extrinsic nominalism, its "signs and insignia" (202). In a similar fashion, the sovereign medal or coin invests the body of the King with the dimensions of a "monarchic host, uniting his image and his deeds, his name and story in a piece of gold or silver" (220), thus providing presence only in the name of power. Both portrait and medal inscribe within their iconic representation a "remainderless" currency. By erasing all traces of the King's private body, these portraits remain iconic allegories.

The traces these medals efface in the public domain, however, remain a real issue within the royal household; the remainder which the portrait and medal erase surfaces as the "pathetic body of the King" in *The Medical Diary of Louis XIV*, dating from the period between 1647 and 1711 and kept by his three court physicians, Vallot, d'Aquin and Fagon. Marin claims that the secret "secreted" in this diary presents a different history of the royal body: "What is exposed here is not a dazzling body, but one that has been purged and bled, one worked over according to the art of the doctor, the historian of what cannot be said, what may not be made visible to all, what may find no public inscription" (221). In the diary, Marin locates a secret and hidden body, subject to the body's dissoluteness, to its unstaunchable secretions and excretions, for Louis XIV had "inherited" his father's disposition to chronic diarrhea which left him "particularly weak in the stomach" (224) and bowels. Marin sees the physician's diary as an attempt to staunch the secretions that threatened the iconic image of the King's glorious body: "The function of the doctor is to clean and tidy up the [screen] story by story, to guarantee and present its absolute transparency. The story of the King's diarrhea which lasted eight months with its occasional symptoms of dysentery and mesenteritis, is particularly striking in this respect, because it allows the reader to witness the very act and event that intertwine the two bodies of the King" (223). Fully apparent in this journal passage is the process of "sublimating the natural body into the historical one, of transforming the former, a body governed by the rhythms of indigestion and dejection, into the latter, a body held under the sway of desire, the will, and glory" (223–4). While Vallot, the physician, was able to bring the King's diarrhea under some form of control in 1653, he was at a loss two years later, with another kind of flow from the royal body. This time, the King was plagued by an inexplicable seminal flow which soiled his shirt with a mixture of "yellow and green." Vallot's attempt to control this flux is another indication of sublimation. Vallot spoke insistently of pursuing a treatment which eventually cleared up the problem, but his diary remains a discourse which attempted to efface the natural and ailing body in a "wholesale and monumental manner" (227).

What remains a private document of the King's illness becomes, in the physician's diary, an intersection of public and private dimensions. As Marin explains: "The historical writings that describe a material body, opaque with all the heaviness incumbent upon flesh, with all the viscosity of blood and humors, with the natural and organic life of the King, this historiography must remain quite private. Only the King has the right to contemplate the body articulated by means of medical signs and symbols and fashioned through the writings of the doctors; only his Majesty has the power to think of himself as a body made of flesh and blood" (230). However, the physician's document presents a different perspective. It is not so much a record of the King's Majesty's ailing body as a testimony of his own skill as physician. Thus the book presents itself not only "as an account of the history of the King's health" but as "a book that exalts the doctor's know-how, his science and his perfect mastery: the specialized servant appropriates for his own benefit the glory of the master." By assuming that, at some point in the future, the diary "may be read as a book of history," Vallot "invents a future public for the diary" (231). This intersection of private and public discourses makes Vallot's diary an interesting example of the iconic sublimation of thing to sign.

If the early diary of Vallot effects a "remainderless exchange," the later medical diary of Louis XIV, kept by physician Fagon, makes the pathetic body of the King an unequivocal "remainder" of the royal exchange. Unlike Vallot, who sweeps the ailing body under the royal rug, Fagon makes the King's ailment the essence of his portrait; by grounding the King's appearance in his "melancholic humour," Fagon makes the pathetic body the point of departure. Thus the ideal body is formed by reference to the natural body; the King is marked by an "apathetic pathos, in terms of a melancholia," which characterizes "the King's natural and physical body"; by doing so, Fagon "equates [this natural body] with the divine body belonging to the heroes of history and myth" (241). Fagon's acknowledgment of this "remainder," this "hidden body," becomes the basis of a second reading of a second form of exchange – the symbolic "exchange" Marin locates in the historical medal commemorating the King's recovery from illness at Calais in 1658. This medal, prepared forty years after the King's recovery, was a commemoration of the King's cure, but, as Marin indicates, it is also a commemoration of the King's illness: "by implication and presupposition," the representation of "the goddess Health is suggestive of an anterior site of illness. The same can be said of the representation of the term *convalescent* (from *convalesco*), meaning to grow, gain strength, recover from an illness" (233). Thus the medal's legend "underscore[s] the identification of the royal body with that of the kingdom" by "[playing] upon both senses of *salus* and *imperium*." "*Salus Imperii*," the health of the supreme power, becomes "*salus Imperii*," the health of the area "where this supreme power is exercised." The health of the King becomes the health of the kingdom or the body politic. The body of King Louis is the political body of France. This symbolic transformation is made possible because the "absolute" has "inscribed within itself a split, an imbalance or failing." The medal's legend is at once the "trace and the expression of this movement of differentiation and identification" (234). The historical medal of 1694 commemorating the King's recovery from illness in 1658 is therefore an instance of transubstantiation. By effecting a double discourse, neither component of which is erased in expression, the medal becomes a symbol of the Incarnate Word.

Marin's location of double discourse within the King's body offers "food for thought" for Carlyle's manipulation of the royal body in *The French Revolution*. Like Fagon, Carlyle identifies French history with an ailing royal body. Louis XV was "arrested at Metz by a malady which threatened to cut short his days" (*W*, 2:1). Thirty years later, the great Prince Louis XVI "again lies sick" (*W*, 2:2); his illness subjects the royal body and kingdom to relentless dissolution. In effect, the royal body is seized by an unstaunchable flux. The text likewise flows with fury. Displacing the Eucharistic incarnation of the body politic – "*L'État c'est moi*" (*W*, 2:9) – with the "cloaca" of the deficit, raging sansculottism, and revolutionary rhetoric, Carlyle presents the "pathetic body" of the King in the throes of a political and semiotic revolution. Paris becomes an emblem of excess "flooded with pamphlets"; it becomes a "[h]ot deluge, – so many Patriot ready-writers, all at the *fervid* or boiling point; each ready-writer, now in the hour of eruption, going like an Iceland Geyser!" (*W*, 2:94). As well, the nation is deluged with paper currency, "GROWN ELECTRIC" (*W*, 2:127) with patriotic enthusiasm; the tocsin sounded from the steeples of the nation becomes the foamy *toxin* of patriotic fervour: "Paris is in the streets; – rushing, foaming like some Venice wine-glass into which you had dropped poison. The tocsin, by order, is pealing madly from all steeples" (*W*, 2:180). The same foaming impetus can be seen in the siege of the Bastille, during which Paris reached the "acme of its frenzy; whirled, all ways, by panic madness." The siege is described as a royal body dissolved by unmanageable flux; the "high-frowning" labyrinthine Mass of the Bastille is besieged at "every street-barricade" by "whirls simmering a minor whirlpool, – strengthening the barricade," and "all minor whirlpools play distractedly into the grand Fire-Mahlstrom which is lashing around the Bastille" (*W*, 2:191). Everywhere, in the pealing of the tocsin, in the flow of arms, in the "[e]lectoral rhetoric" (*W*, 2:206) of a hapless Saint-Antoine, in the eddying vortex of violence, Carlyle sees the royal body made dissolute by ailing secretions. The metaphor of the royal body dissolves in metamorphosis: "Vanished is the Bastille, what we call vanished: the *body*, or sandstones, of it hanging, in benign metamorphosis, for centuries to come" (*W*, 2:209).

In its metamorphosis, the Bastille becomes an intersection of private and public spaces; the iconic imperatives of the old feudal order, dependent so much on the sublimation of a diseased and private body to the glorified and public body, are dissolved by a "secretion" determined to move beyond the secretive to the public arena. In his description of the siege as *publication* of a Bastille whose plan at one point defied human understanding, Carlyle makes the event a site of disclosure. The Bastille, which has preserved its secretive passages from discovery, is made the "Ordnance of all calibres" by "men of all plans" (*W*, 2:191). Every man becomes "his own engineer" in making public a fortress which has so far remained immune from conspicuous consumption; the patriots subject the private body of the ancien regime to market display: after the siege, "[c]rowds of the curious roam through its caverns" to gaze on the "skeletons found walled-up" in their iron cages (*W*, 2:209).

Carlyle's manipulation of the pathetic body in *The French Revolution* underscores the problematic status of representation within the ailing French kingship. The glorious body of the King fails as a symbol of French nationhood; yet the patriot's struggle to spawn a "Revolutionary Prodigy" is equally disastrous. The "Revolutionary Prodigy" becomes, in Carlyle's words, the discrepancy between paper ideal and actuality: "unfolding itself into terrific stature and articulation, by its own laws and Nature's, not by the laws of Formula," it has become "unintelligible, incredible as an impossibility, the 'waste chaos of a Dream' ... a kind of Nightmare Vision ... disowned by the Laws of Nature and of Formula" (*W*, 4:138). The revolutionary prodigy is the unreadable text of a newly articulated Constitution based on Rousseau's *Social Contract*.

Rousseau strips the glorious body from the French King and reinvests it in the body politic; his contract creates a "fictitious person endowed with certain faculties, active like the sovereign, passive like the state."[3] Paul de Man refers to this strategy as a form of "metaphorical totalization"[4] which Rousseau is unable to sustain when he attempts to elaborate on the practical logistics of his social contract. For de Man, Rousseau's text is divided against itself; it remains a pathetic body despite Rousseau's attempt to effect a "remainderless exchange" between the people and the state. De Man dissolves the "remarkably smooth and homogenous surface of the *Social Contract*" (248) by underscoring the discrepancy between political theory and political action.

An example of this discrepancy occurs in the formal definition of the social contract. Using the first version of the *Social Contract* (known as the "manuscript de Genève") as basis, de Man argues for Rousseau's rejection of a natural principle of totalization as the foundation of sound political organization: "Hence, the categorical rejection, more explicit in the early version than in the final text, of the family as a suitable political model, precisely because the family is based on natural ties" (260). Yet, the formal definition of the contract which emphasizes the synecdochic relationship of part to whole and which promises to "[unite] limb to body, one to all, individual to group" (259) "seems to relapse into the figure [of totalization] which has just been decisively condemned" (261). Another example of such discrepancy occurs in the context of the "thieving lawmaker" (270) who assumes the dimension of the "sovereign" whom Rousseau has categorically rejected in book 1. "[N]o man has any natural authority over his fellows," Rousseau writes, yet he insists that his lawgiver cannot be an ordinary man, for the "lawgiver's great soul is the true miracle which must vindicate his mission."[5] Further indication of a text that goes against itself is seen in the paradox emerging from the relationship between the individual and the collective body. Rousseau claims for this relationship a "remainderless exchange": "as the sovereign is formed entirely of the individuals who compose it, it has not, nor could it have, any interest contrary to theirs; and so the sovereign has no need to give guarantees to the subjects, because it is impossible for a body to wish to hurt all of its members and ... it cannot hurt any particular member. The sovereign by the mere fact that it is, is always all that it ought to be."[6] De Man, however, reveals the instability of this exchange. Within the social contract, each individual is committed to a double relationship, to himself and to the collective state; the state, however, in its executive position as sovereign, remains "in-dividual, un-divided." The individual is marked by "two distinct rhetorical models, the first self-reflexive or specular, the other estranged." Thus the individual is estranged from his own executive power, his sovereign, because "this power is unlike him and foreign to him"; it does not have "the same double and self-contradictory structure and therefore does not share in his problems and tensions" (de Man, *Allegories*, 265). Far from creating a sovereign power acting on behalf of the people, the social contract promotes and is promoted by an incipient contradiction between the people and the state.

Both Carlyle and de Man locate these contradictions in the social contract within a discrepancy between political theory and action. But while Carlyle complains bitterly of unfit readers, de Man sees these political contradictions as part of a larger reality, as the necessary linguistic impasse imposed on man by "a fact of language" (277). Thus the implicit displacement of the individual by the state, the particular by the general, becomes, in de Man's terms, the displacement of "referential meaning" by a "grammatical" or "legal text." "As a text," writes de Man, "the *Social Contract* is unusual among Rousseau's works because of its impersonal, machine like systematicity; it takes a few key terms, programs a relationship between them and lets mere syntax take its course" (268). In its suppression of the particular, in its suspension of referential meaning, the *Social Contract* becomes a text whose "logic of grammar" betrays itself; thus "the text can be considered as the theoretical description of the state, considered as a contractual and legal model, but also as the disintegration of this same model as soon as it is put in motion" (271). The *Social Contract* is therefore an "allegory of unreadability"; "it persists in performing what it has shown to be impossible to do" (275).

From de Man's perspective, a text that promises what it cannot deliver becomes the failure not of the reader but of the word. De Man's approach to the text allows us, at least, to see that history is not so much the bias of the will as the bias of a "thieving" language. If history is indeed generated by "rhetorical complexity" (277), then the participants of the French Revolution were not so much doomed by lack of foresight as by the ambiguity of language itself. If indeed all texts simultaneously assert and deny the "authority of [their] own rhetorical mode" (17), Carlyle's *French Revolution* becomes not only an allegory of reading but an "allegory of unreadability" (247) as well. Carlyle's text valorizes "process" over the formulaic reading of the philosophes; yet in this confrontation between process and formula, he places the latter within a context upon which the former is dependent. Without being placed in opposition to formulas, processes exemplified in the Noetic Pentad, processes inherent in the evolutionary ethos of the French Revolution would have been meaningless. Carlyle's text challenges the transparency of allegory, yet it validates, in this pursuit, that which it denounces. The parodic placed beside the sacramental affirms the contiguity and necessity of both. In this sense, Robespierre defines Napoleon, for the latter can only be "heroicized" through the failure of the former. *The French Revolution* never manages, even in Napoleon, to resurrect for itself a truly heroic figure. We never see Napoleon in the front; he hovers as a peripheral figure throughout the text because Carlyle understands that what he makes acute in Napoleon can never achieve the dimensions of central discourse. Once he does that, Napoleon becomes another formula. Napoleon can only be seen in the periphery, in the way that the symbol can only be a projected vision, looming in the distance, never fully coming into focus or dying off early, as did our friend and prototype, Mirabeau. If Carlyle argues for the symbol's pre-eminence, he does so only by making it an embedded text or voice like Goethe's commentary, grafted to the final section of *The*

French Revolution. While the revolutionary shrieks in its wake, the symbol has never been more than bated breath.

Carlyle's symbol is played out as a metaphorical text which cannot be validated within the discourse of its history; hence the ending with Cagliostro, a totally metaphorical character expounding on a metaphorical prophecy. The final section of the *history* of the French Revolution becomes a metalepsis or substitution – a prophecy prophesied *"ex postfacto"* by a fictional character, the Arch Quack, Cagliostro. Even New France in the final chapter remains, at best, a potential: "The new Realities are not yet come: ah no, only Phantasms, Paper models, tentative Prefigurements of such!" (W, 4:322). What we are asked to understand is that the symbol can only be perceived, like the Last Judgment, as a suspended "reality"; it cannot be wholly realized in the text that prefigures it. *The French Revolution* therefore can never be more than prefigurement. From De Man's perspective, such prefigurement is tantamount to lying; like the *Social Contract*, *The French Revolution* can only promise without being able to carry out its promises. The economy of the symbol is itself a linguistic paradox: it transcends the economics of the word, yet remains suspended within its idiom. As de Man states, "The two readings have to engage each other in direct confrontation, for the one reading is precisely the error denounced by the other and had to be undone by it"; yet, neither "can exist in the other's absence" (12).

The King's pathetic body is ratified by a medallion that celebrates his *recovery* from private illness; the iconic royal body depends on the pathetic body for its representation. Perhaps the word "recovery" is the most viable term to describe the necessary "doubleness" within language. On the road to recovery, but not quite whole, lies the seed of the symbol. The economy can never displace the economics of the word. If the former transcends the latter, it can only do so with the understanding that, without the grammar of economic realities, we might never have a glimpse of the economy that is not quite here, but yet to be. In "Characteristics," Carlyle speaks of the illness attendant on a self-conscious France: "The Self-consciousness is the symptom merely; nay, it is also the attempt towards cure" (W, 28:20). In a later period of his life, coming to terms with the illness of his middle years, Carlyle writes:

Other things might have made me hopeful and cheerful as beseemed my years, – had not *Dyspepsia*, with its base and unspeakable miseries, kept such fatal hold of me, which perhaps, needed only a *wise* Doctor, too, as I found afterwards, when too late! Heavy, grinding, and continual has that burden lain on me ever since to this hour, and will lie; but I must not complain of it, either; it was not wholly a *curse*, as I can sometimes recognize, but perhaps a thing needed, and partly a *blessing*, though a stern one, and bitter to flesh and blood. (*TNB*, 57n2)

5 Afterword: *Sordello* and the Economics of Representation

Parallels between Carlyle's *The French Revolution* and Browning's *Sordello* have been the focus of some critical attention in recent years. Mark Cumming, for example, perceives a connection between the dense and resistant prose in *The French Revolution* and the "brother's speech" in book 5 of *Sordello*.[1] Similarly, David E. Latané views Carlyle and Browning as direct inheritors of the Romantic paradigm of "fit audience, though few." Their places in this tradition contribute to what Latané calls an "aesthetics of difficulty." Latané's exploration of Browning's linguistic density and its concomitant demands on the reader situates the poem within a Romantic preoccupation with "select readership."[2] Citing Dryden, Milton, and Coleridge as precursors, Latané gives this readership an "apostolic" flavour; even though the "fit audience" is a small one, it can effect larger ambitions; it can generate a democratization of values such that the fit and few readers can eventually expand into the "People." Distinction between the "Public" and the "People" is therefore crucial to Romantic poetics. Latané claims that Wordsworth's characterization of the "People" is to some degree abstracted; opposed to the "Public," "[the People] carries democratic"[3] and eventually universal connotations. The "fit but few" is the beginning of a genuine and universal brotherhood. Given this apostolic imperative, the poet becomes the creator and generator of a community of initiates.

What I plan to pursue in this chapter is not so much an extension of as a corollary to Latané's commendably thorough exploration of Browning's aesthetics of incomprehensibility. What I will examine is

Browning's adoption of a "money" economy to circumscribe a linguistic problem; in setting up Sordello as an abstracted "god-term," Browning poses before his readers the problem of representation. In this sense, *Sordello* is a crisis of kingship, specifically within the Carlylean context of "aggregative" rather than synecdochic representation. This aggregative principle is most thoroughly expressed in Browning's depiction of Sordello's "crowd," which functions throughout the poem as Sordello's attempt at finding material expression for his soul. This attempt, however, is foiled at every turn, not because the crowd is resistant, but because Sordello, like Marat and Robespierre, is dominated by a fixed imperative – a Manichean vision of soul and body as dualistic and mutually exclusive entities so that a genuinely dialectical union cannot be generated from the opposition. Sordello's attempt at kingship, at representing the crowd, can generate only a "counterfeit" economy. In book 1, for example, he creates for entertainment a "crowd" of "puppets his crude phantasy / Supposes notablest – popes, kings, priests, knights."[4] Browning compares this "sudden company" (1:784) with "counterfeit" currency:

> ... Once care because such make account,
> Allow that foreign recognitions stamp
> The current value, and his crowd shall vamp
> Him counterfeits enough; and so their print
> Be on the piece, 'tis gold, attests the mint,
> And "good," pronounce they whom his new appeal
> Is made to: if their casual print conceal –
> This arbitrary good of theirs o'ergloss
> What he has lived without, nor felt the loss –
> Qualities strange, ungainly, wearisome,
> What matter? (1:786–96)

The "crowd" Sordello fancies is seen as paper substitutes for gold, arbitrary proxies of genuine human relationships. What matter, Sordello rationalizes, if he deals exclusively with arbitrary signifiers? What matter if his "creations" are a "pageant" – a "marshalled flock / Of authorized enjoyments" (1:806–7), merely a means of displaying sovereign authorship? In espousing a "counterfeit" economy at Goito, Sordello remains, as yet, an untested sovereign, a king of "pipe dreams." His representation of the people remains similarly mythological.

Again, in book 4, Sordello contemplates the crowd as a "new body" he has taken on to express his soul; he hopes to "become eventually whole / With them as he had hoped to be without" (4:204–5); but what transpires in his association with the crowd is something less than anticipated:

> And the new body, ere he could suspect,
> Cohered, mankind and he were really fused,
> The new self seemed impatient to be used
> By him, but utterly another way
> Than that anticipated: strange to say,
> They were too much below him, more in thrall
> Than he, the adjunct than the principal.
> What booted scattered units? – here a mind
> And there, which repay his own to find,
> And stamp, and use? (4:250–9)

More "adjunct than the principal," the crowd is not so much a "brotherhood" as a conglomeration of scattered units – here and there a few followers whose loyalty comes not from a genuine interaction with their leader but from blind obedience. Browning again likens Sordello's relationship with these scattered followers to the "stamp" and "use" of paper currency.

Browning's primary concern in the depiction of Goito is the establishment of an allegorical bias. This can be seen in the description of Goito as a spot "reclaimed" from the "surrounding spoil" (1:380). A place so "bound" (1:383) and "captured" (1:384) that it "precludes distress" (1:385), Goito mirrors the contractarian world of benevolence exposed in *The French Revolution*. The "contracted" world of Goito is suggested by Browning's portrayal of the caryatides on the font as "noiseless girls" (1:424) who, "having ... once drunk sweetness to the dregs" (1:427), are now "resigned" (1:426) forever to do penance. In the sense that these girls are bound by a "contract" of penance, Sordello is equally bound by the "contract" of salvation. He perceives his visits to the font as a means of redemption; "constant as eve he came" (1:429) to beg pardon for these indebted maidens as if his presence provides somehow a form of absolution. Browning describes Sordello's self-idealizing posture in terms of the refining of gold. Refusing to leave until he sees "[s]unset slant cheerful through the buttress-chinks" (1:433), Sordello convinces himself that he is an efficacious agent of redemption; his visits retrieve the shafts of a setting sun into "Gold seven times globed" (1:434), a reference to the refinement of gold into globules. A god-term like gold, he discharges the "debt" of the penanced girls by lightening their "load" and erasing their "stain" (1:436). Yet the absolution remains an allegory at best because the debt is not really discharged nor the sinners redeemed. Sordello leaves the girls to "linger out the penance in mute stone" (1:442), only to repeat the fantasy at his next visit. The font therefore enacts the Apollonian myth of author as founding and redeeming subject, a god-term whose imperative for eternity and perfection consigns language to the speechlessness of a Grecian urn. Privileging eternity over time, Sordello places Goito within a Manichean rivalry; because eternity is the "mastery" of "another life" (1:565), he is unable to "[stoop]" (1:556) to the "world's occasion" (1:559) which he considers "worthless since / Not absolutely fitted to evince / [this] mastery" (1:559–61). The author as redeeming subject is given to us in book 1 as "Apollo's gaze" (1:962), the fixed imperative of an abstracted and abstracting consciousness. Two passages specifically emphasize this.

The first can be seen in Browning's description of Sordello's crowd. The immaterial nature of this crowd is suggested when Browning states that it is composed of qualities Sordello has abstracted from the "entire out-world" (1:757):

Strength, wisdom, grace on every hand
Soon disengaged themselves, and he discerned
A sort of human life: at least, was turned
A stream of lifelike figures through his brain.
Lord, liegeman, valvassor and suzerain,
Ere he could choose, surrounded him; a stuff
To work his pleasure on; there, sure enough:
But as for gazing, what shall fix that gaze?
Are they to simply testify the ways
He who convoked them sends his soul along
With the cloud's thunder or a dove's brood-song?
– While they live each his life ...   (1:764–75)

Browning suggests that these creations are abstractions of Sordello himself; they stand as mute reflections of an author who can generate only *self*, not *other*. Not quite "human," his figures stand as spectral substitutes. Sordello's "drowsy Paradise" (1:627) is an "artless wonder" (1:385), "Secure beside in its own loveliness" (1:386), but unable to participate in the flesh and blood world of men and time. What emerges from "Goito's crypt" is not the "fiery thrill" of heroic action but "blank issue" (6:338–9).

The second passage which emphasizes the abstracted state of Goito can be seen in Browning's discussion of the meaning of love for a "being" like Sordello. If Sordello is indeed "foremost in that regal class / Nature has broadly severed from her mass / Of men, and framed for pleasure" (1:467–9), then "[h]ow can such love?" (1:483). This question is the key to an understanding of the poem, for what Browning develops through the course of the six books is the idea that abstractions, like Sordello, cannot love, cannot participate genuinely in the "world's occasion" because an abstracting consciousness is necessarily dualistic. In book 6, Browning ascribes Sordello's failure to his inability to accept a power which "utterly incomprehensible / Is out of rivalry, which thus you can / Love, though unloving all conceived by man" (6:591–4). Sordello's inability to go beyond a Manichean "rivalry" prevents him from participating in this "incomprehensible" love. At Goito, Sordello's "love" takes the form of self-idolatry; he makes of the beloved (the external world) a mirror reflection of his soul by

> [proclaiming] each new revealment born a twin
> With a distinctest consciousness within,
> Referring still the quality, now first
> Revealed, to [his] own soul – its instinct nursed
> In silence, now remembered better, shown
> More thoroughly, but not the less [his] own;
> A dream come true ... (1:525–31)

Browning suggests that Sordello is unable to love in the genuine sense because he has not moved beyond the realm of allegories. If the other exists only as an affirmation of self, then Sordello's reading of the external world is a necessarily delusive one. His Apollonian position as the god-term separated from the world of Nature, which "nature [was] prest / At eve to worship" (1:926–7), allows him only to "spawn" himself in the act of authoring. "Thrusting in time eternity's concern" (1:566), privileging the latter as the arena for the soul, Sordello is Coleridge's "real opposition"; the result is the absent text. Indeed, Sordello's failure to generate his "text" at Goito is repeated twice during the course of the poem – in his departure from Mantua and in his final demise. Despite Browning's claim that the significant features of the poem lie in the "incidents in the development of a soul,"[5] Goito remains a "contracted house" (*Sordello*, 1:587), an indelible impress on Sordello's soul which ironically prevents him from making the creative leap into the world of action. "Whom palled Goito with its perfect things?" asks Browning in book 6; he promptly replies: "Sordello's self: whereas for Mankind springs / Salvation by each hindrance interposed" (6:273–6). It is the currency of the privileged signifier, the abstracted god-term at Goito, that prevents

Sordello from becoming what Carlyle terms the "prophetic" reader.

Sordello's career as people's poet in Mantua stands as a "hindrance" which he seeks to neutralize rather than labour through in a genuine attempt at salvation. Doting on public support after his defeat of Eglamor at the competition, Sordello sacrifices labour for popularity; he writes not for the "song itself" (2:486), but for the crowd's "sterling happiness" (2:507). Soon disenchanted, however, with being an adjunct to public opinion, he makes a "[f]ond essay" (2:587) at forging a distinctive and genuine language, to body forth the "imaged thing" (2:571). The result is a new experimental language which Browning refers to as a "rude / Armour" (2:576-7) hammered out into a "creature" (2:584), which Sordello proceeds to "equip" with "limbs in harness of his workmanship" (2:585-6). The remodelled language, however, fails because the crowd cannot understand it. Sordello realizes that "perceptions whole, like that he sought / To clothe, reject so pure a work of thought / As language" (2:589-91); what he conceives as "perception whole," the seamless fabric of eternity, cannot be articulated by a language that comes under the strictures of time; the whole, he concludes, cannot be presented by parts, "the simultaneous and the sole / By the successive and the many" (2:594-5). He compares his attempt at forging a genuine language to "playing there what happened here / And occupied abroad by what he spurned / At home" (2:736-8). While Sordello can be commended for recognizing the paradox implicit in language, his failure lies in his inability to go beyond this paradox. Reading the crowd's rejection as an insoluble rivalry between eternity and time, himself and the people, Sordello chooses the easy solution; instead of labouring further towards a genuine language of the people, he returns to the old paradigm of appeasement: "they with the old verse / And [he] with the old praise" (2:609-10). What might have become a scene of prophetic reading, what might have become an occasion for dialectical generation, becomes in this instance an absent or allegorical text. His Mantuan attempts at writing were all abortive failures; unable to accept *both* eternity and time within the context of a prophetic Imaginary, Sordello swings from one position to the other. The result is inactivity:

> If dreams were tried,
> His will swayed sicklily from side to side,
> Nor merely neutralized his waking act
> But tended e'en in fancy to distract
> The intermediate will, the choice of means.
> He lost the art of dreaming ... (2:845-50)

Sundered in two, each half unable to accommodate the other, Sordello exists as a neutralized third term. This is most clearly reflected in his return to Goito at the end of book 2. Asked to "sound" (2:928) Taurello's return to Mantua, Sordello, mute as "stone" (2:938), retreats to a familiar paradigm of inaction – the font at Goito. There, he crowns himself – "I shall be king again" (2:1001) – an action which, within the context of his withdrawal, is an ironic commentary on his position as sovereign signifier.

If Goito stands as the arbitrary signifier, the part which can never be whole because it is subsumed by an allegorical imperative, Ferrara stands as the motivated signifier, the part which can be whole because it is able to build from the shreds and patches of humanity a genuine community of interest. If Sordello's font at Goito is an emblem of a "contracted" consciousness, Salinguerra's laver at Ferrara is an emblem of a synecdochic and holistic immersion in the world of action. Unlike the compound at Goito, Salinguerra's castle and grounds are sites of unextinguished energy. The trees are not confining rings, as they are in Goito, hiding "their main defiles" (1:383) and "[binding] the rest" (1:383-4). Instead, each tree on Salinguerra's grounds "grew as it contrived" (4:117); like "tamed lions" (4:119), they stand not as neutralized but rechannelled energy. While Goito is "some captured creature in a pound" (1:384) whose vigour has been suppressed by an artificial bid for peace, the "tamed lions," like the "uneasy leopards' heads" (4:128) supporting the laver, suggest energy on the threshold of expression. The same energy characterizes the "range of statues" (4:141) which the narrator purposefully contrasts to the caryatides of the font at Goito:

> only these [at Ferrara]
> Are up and doing; not abashed, a troop
> Able to right themselves – who see you, stoop
> Their arms o'the instant after you.   (4:148–51)

The laver at Ferrara stands as a synecdoche of the world of action. Its owner, Salinguerra, is similarly imbued with representational power, for Browning makes Salinguerra part of a whole:

> ... in Romana sought he wife and child
> And for Romana's sake seemed reconciled
> To losing individual life, which shrunk
> As the other prospered – mortised in his trunk;
> Like a dwarf palm which wanton Arabs foil
> Of bearing its own proper wine and oil,

> By grafting into it the stranger-vine,
> Which sucks its heart out, sly and serpentine,
> Till forth one vine-palm feathers to the root,
> And old drops moisten the insipid fruit. (4:556–65)

Browning renders the synecdochic potential of Salinguerra in horticultural terms: the grafting of a "stranger vine" onto the dwarf palm which, by preventing the limited use of self-pollination, forces the plant to produce beyond its self-generating capacity. The grafted plant can generate new growth; unlike Ecelin, whose brain atrophied because "his old palm-stock / Endured no influx of strange strengths" (4:642–3), the dwarf palm is strengthened by alien influence. Like the "Alien turning Native" (3:167–8) and extending the boundaries of the native soil, the grafted vine is an emblem of communion as an ever-widening circle of assimilation. Even Sordello recognizes this principle of growth: "Let essence, whatsoe'er it be," he claims "extend – / Never contract" (5:532–3). As we shall see, what he comprehends in spirit is never transmuted into action. Ferrara stands, a city dismembered by war, but able to regenerate from its agony a genuine community of interest. This can be seen in Browning's description of Sordello's second entrance:

> Into Ferrara – not the empty town
> That morning witnessed: he went up and down
> Streets whence the veil had been stript shred by shred,
> So that, in place of huddling with their dead
> Indoors, to answer Salinguerra's ends,
> Townsfolk make shift to crawl forth, sit like friends
> With any one. (4:337–42)

After the bloodshed, Ferrara is left in fragments, but not in despair, for groups are assembling in the aftermath to hear the "Leaguer's mass" (4:350), to salvage an unbeaten sense of brotherhood by calling for Sordello, their minstrel, to articulate their need for forgiveness and peace (4:356–61). It is with this vision of Ferrara that Sordello is asked to become the "incarnation of the People's hope" (4:381).

Ferrara is an emblem of the "incarnate word," the third term generated, not neutralized, by war. It stands as the only sign of hope which, emerging "out of rivalry," is capable of dialectical regeneration. This third term can be seen as well in Browning's reference to Rome in the Crescentius Nomentanus episode and in Sordello's temporary bid for rebuilding Rome. Implicit in these two episodes is the vision of a new Rome to supplant the political and linguistic stalemate confronting Sordello. Faced with what he deems an insoluble conflict between the Guelf and Ghibellin factions, Sordello in book 4 asks for an alternative course of action:

> Two parties take the world up, and allow
> No third, yet have one principle, subsist
> By the same injustice; whoso shall enlist
> With either, ranks with man's inveterate foes.
> So there is one less quarrel to compose:
> The Guelf, the Ghibellin may be to curse –
> I have done nothing, but both sides do worse
> Than nothing. Nay, to me, forgotten, reft
> Of insight, lapped by trees and flowers, was left
> The notion of a service – ha? What lured
> Me here, what mighty aim was I assured
> Must move Taurello? What if there remained
> A cause, intact, distinct from these, ordained
> For me, its true discoverer? (4:939–52)

This third principle, "out of rivalry," is what Sordello the visionary is able to see but not effect. In this sense, Crescentius Nomentanus is the prototype of Sordello, for he too fails to realize an alternative vision. Crescentius Nomentanus was a Roman consul who wanted to restore the vanished Republic of Rome. Pitted against both Emperor and Pope, both ecclesiastical and secular authorities, he was the third principle who was unfortunately crucified in the "rivalry." Browning's depiction of Crescentius Nomentanus is resistant and obscure; he couches the story within a brother's speech – a brother who claims to sing the ballad of Crescentius whenever the superior introduces a novice in order to underscore the Manichean tensions the vow of celibacy creates within the context of Christian brotherhood. Focusing on his "merry" appointment to the brotherhood until Pope Innocent "bade [him] relinquish, to [his] small content, / [his] wife or [his] brown sleeves" (4:967–8), the brother makes a subtle indictment of the Church's hostility towards the secular realm. This brother's speech points to the "blank issue" of such rivalry: "I had the option to keep wife / Or keep brown sleeves, and managed in the strife / Lose both" (4:998–1000). The third principle is given to us in yet another analogy in book 4 – in the vision of Saint Francis as the viable alternative to both the Crusade and the League for "[coalescing] the small and the great" (5:189), that is, as a means of bonding or brotherhood. Both the Crusade "or trick of breeding Strength by other aid / than Strength" (5:196–7) and the League or "trick of turning Strength / Against Pernicious Strength" (5:199–200) maintain strength (or physical force) as the principal source of community. Only Saint Francis, "preaching peace / Yonder! God's truce – or trick to supersede / The very use of Strength" (5:202–4), carves the way for the future so that the hero of the "next age" (5:205) can bring the third principle into fruition "gourd-like ... not the flower's display / Nor the root's prowess, but the plenteous way / O' the plant" (5:207–9). Saint Francis belongs to that incomprehensible power because his is a genuine brotherhood based not on strength but on love. It is this brotherhood which forges relationships among men here and now and in the generations to come; it is this brotherhood which can be read as a link between this age and the next and as the foundation of a new Rome. This brotherhood is, moreover, the basis of a viable author-reader relationship, the "brother's speech" which Sordello comes close to articulating.

Sordello is given the vision of this new Rome, but he is unwilling to make this vision prophetic. At the end of book 5, Taurello throws him the badge, making him Romano's Head. Sordello, left alone in the chamber to consider the position, goes through the same internal struggle he experienced in Mantua just before his return to the font. This time, however, Sordello recognizes the duplicity implicit in Goito: "Goito's vines / Stand like a cheat detected" (5:1017–18). Betrayed by an allegorical kingship, he is unable to assume genuine sovereignty when political power is placed in his hands. Dominated by the god-term Apollo, he is unable to surrender himself to an "[e]xternal power" (6:111), the moon, whose influence would have brought him out of himself into an authentic interaction with the world. Reduced by the Apollonian vision to a token of power, Sordello stands like a "gilt / Shield in the sunshine" (6:52–3), a "place / For much display; not gathered up and, hurled / Right from its heart, encompassing the world" (6:54–6). In Carlylean terms, Sordello is reduced to a "scenic Nation," all galvanic motion, but impotent to act. Thus he can only envy those who, while they do not possess half his strength, yet are able to "[submit] to some moon, before / Them still" and are "able therefore to fulfil a course, / Nor missed life's crown, authentic attribute" (6:60–3). This sovereignty Sordello is unable to assume; unwilling to seek the whole by parts, he relinquishes the world of action; now that he has "found that Whole, / Could [he] revert, enjoy past gains?" (6:284–5). Unwilling to attempt "communication different," Sordello fails to become a motivated signifier, to be the genuine incarnation and symbol of his people. His consumption by a "moneyed" imperative prevents him from effecting a material expression of his vision. If genuine communication involves a "communion of souls," Sordello fails because his "[p]erception [brooding] unexpressed and whole" (5:436) remains undigested. "A healthy spirit like a healthy frame / Craves aliment in plenty," the narrator writes, but this aliment is digested by the body which "[c]hanges, assimilates its aliment" (5:437–9) into food. It is only from such digestion that new growth can be effected:

'Tis Knowledge, whither such perceptions tend;
They lose themselves in that, means to an end,
The many old producing some one new,
A last unlike the first. (5:443–6).

Sordello, however, does not "digest" his vision, for "[n]ext day no formularies more you saw / Than figs or olives in a sated maw" (5:441–2); "a meal" of "munched millet grains and lettuce leaves / Together in his stomach rattle loose" (5:448–9). Undigested, unprocessed, his vision remains "blank issue," part of the consuming imperative of allegory. Naddo asks Sordello to "supply a famished world" (2:476–7); Sordello's songs, however, provide not real food but phantom proxies.

"What has Sordello found?" Browning asks, "Or can his spirit go the mighty round / End where poor Eglamor began?" (6:604–6). Sordello, who supersedes Eglamor in book 2, ends no better than his vanquished predecessor; unlike Dante who is able to "take the next step, next age" (5:206) and triumph over a precursor text, Sordello goes the "mighty round" like Blake's self-ingesting primates who are unable to make the creative leap out of a repetitive currency of ideas. What kind of poet is Eglamor? A poet of least resistance; he sees language as a soothing "rite" (2:203), "mixed / With his own life, unloosed when he should please, / Having it safe at hand, ready to ease / All pain, remove all trouble" (2:206–9). Sordello, therefore, ends not as the voice of prophecy but as the speaker for a logic of general currency. Through Sordello's demise, however, Browning suggests that the prophetic voice is necessarily a difficult and resistant one, the voice least amenable to clean and transparent transcription. In the opening section of *Sordello*, he plays with the notions of authorship and accessibility. He presents the reader with two different kinds of authors and, by implication, two different kinds of readers. The first type of author hides behind his presentation; he tends to "body forth" by "making speak, [himself] kept out of view, / The very man as he was wont to do, / And leaving you to say the rest for him" (1:14–17). This author is invisible for he is "not a whit /

More in the secret than yourselves who sit / Fresh-chapleted to listen" (1:24–6). Such an author allows the reader to reconstruct for himself his understanding of the character's "progress" (1:23). If this author demands reader participation, the second author rejects it; for the author who wants to set forth "unexampled themes" (1:26), a different approach seems necessary; instead of permitting full audience participation, this author

> Would best chalk broadly on each vesture's hem
> The wearer's quality; or take [his] stand,
> Motley on back and pointing-pole in hand,
> Beside him. (1:28–31)

In his provision for an unresistant text, this author functions most like a lecturer. Though Browning claims that he prefers the first type of "authoring" to the second, he feels obliged to adopt the lecturer's stand, since poets who want to be "setters forth of unexampled themes, / Makers of quite new men, producing them" (1:26–7) would best take the path of least resistance. Browning provides his reader with two choices, yet what transpires in *Sordello* is neither one nor the other, but a composite third. What he presents is an author-narrator who gives many editorial directions, but these directions confound, rather than clarify, the issue. The result is an author "not kept out of view," but who nevertheless makes inordinate demands on the reader. The authorial voice which emerges in *Sordello* aims not to please but to obstruct the reader at every turn; he is the kind Browning actually inscribes in book 5 of the text:

> Myself, implied
> Superior now, as by the platform's side,
> I bade them do and suffer, – would last content
> The world ... no – that's too far! I circumvent
> A few, my masque contented, and to these
> Offer unveil the last of mysteries –
> Man's inmost life shall have yet freer play:
> Once more I cast external things away,
> And natures composite, so decompose
> That" ... Why, he writes *Sordello*! (5:611–20)

The author who emerges in this section of the text is one who assumes editorial or narrative "superiority," yet who, despite his explicit manipulation of the characters, "would last content the world," would last make his intentions transparent to his audience.

Considering this last statement to be too extreme a position, Browning interjects and modifies the statement so that the author becomes not one who chooses to content the world, but one who values "song" over "song's effect" by "[offering to] unveil the last of mysteries" only to those deserving few. These few and fit readers he would merely "circumvent" by "[casting] external things away" and decomposing "nature's composite" so that an understanding of the text can be generated only by the reader's participation in rewriting the text. The reader who emerges in this section is a genuine brother who can "[supply]" (5:623) what the author suggests, who, with the author, can supersede the past for the author's word remains "god's germ, doomed to remain a germ / In unexpanded infancy, unless" (3:982-3) the reader labours to be the "supplement" of its expansion. Together, they "talk as brothers talk" (5:625); they participate in a genuine language where "an accent's change gives each / The other's soul – no speech to understand / By former audience" (5:636-8). Each the material expression of the other, author and reader participate in a barter form of communication like the potential but unrealized

> ... Complete Sordello, Man and Bard
> John's cloud-girt Angel, this foot on the land,
> That on the sea, with, open in his hand,
> A bitter-sweeting of a book ...   (2:690-3)

This "Complete Sordello" is Carlyle's phantasmagoric symbol, the heroic incarnation Sordello attempts but fails to effect.

Browning is emphatic that the ideal reader does *not* "reconstruct what stands already" (5:641), but from "the ancient" produces "new structure" (5:643); in effect, the reader is the prophet of a new age who must take "the plenteous way / O' the plant" (5:208-9), who must not wander in repetitive circles, but must take the leap to the "next age." Implicit in this leap is the author's prerogative to "unmask" "Life's elemental masque" (5:584), to "unstation" (5:603) by "communication different" (6:600) "the men and women stationed hitherto" (5:602). The masque, as an emblem of language, embraces the two poles of authorship, as a marshalling and display of characters, an "unreal pageantry / Of essences" (2:564-5), *and* as a dissolution of this pageantry. The poet as masquer can be either a Pageant-Master or a Maker-See; in his distinction between the two, Browning favours the latter, whom he considers the creator of "true works" (3:622). The former understands the author to be a god-term, the "gazer" at the world of action, who "merely make[s] report / The work existed ere

[his] day" (3:923–4). The latter comprehends the author to be "god's germ," whose expansion depends on a "leap from the allotted world" (3:980), a departure from the known and transparent; this is the author who does not merely report, but who "[carries] on a stage / The work o' the world" (3:922–3). If the Pageant-Master says "what it was [he] saw," the Maker-See "[i]mpart[s] the gift of seeing to the rest" (3:867–8) and by doing so leaves an area of freedom "escaped" from the totalitarian imperative of authorship. The Pageant-Master produces "authorized enjoyments" (1:807); like Eglamor's songs in which one finds "completeness" because "song and singer" are one (3:620), the Pageant-Master engenders a repetitive circulation of "self" in his productions. The language of the Maker-See is necessarily resistant to facile reproduction because there "escapes" (3:624) some aspect which cannot be explained; "his lay was but an episode/In the bard's life" (3:629–30), a fragment of the whole. It is this sense of the fragment that forms the basis of Browning's digression; his authorial intrusion into the narrative serves to puncture the notion of time as a seamless and coherent fabric and to reinforce the idea that the language of the Maker-See is necessarily resistant to such "complete" comprehension. Thus when Browning considers making the beggar-girl a "queen," he is playing with the idea of authorial control; by making her a "queen," he is, in effect, framing her within a predetermined text; he is dressing her up for "[p]arade ... for the common credit" (3:733) and "[vouching] / That a luckless residue" usually sent "to crouch / In corners out of sight, was just as framed / For happiness" (3:733–6). Should he make the beggar girl into a "queen," Browning would be extending the totalitarian implications of authorial control. The "framing" author dispenses with the contingencies of life; his peasants and queens, "made happy by whatever means" (3:732), are mere puppets to be controlled by block and pulley. In book 3, Browning beseeches his readers to mutiny against such authors who so presume themselves "god-terms" that they reject the necessary colloquy with their audience; "all you, beneath," Browning urges, "[s]hould scowl at, bruise [the] lips and break [the] teeth" of those "Who ply the pulleys, for neglecting you" (3:931–3). Thus Browning's Paduan girl rejects the easy "tailoring" of a Pageant-Master; she remains a "sad disshevelled ghost" (3:696) whose shreds permit her ironically to "see" with a vision more democratic than that accorded a well-decked man:

> Divide the robe yet farther: be content
> With seeing just a score pre-eminent
> Through shreds of it, acknowledged happy wights,

Engrossing what should furnish all, by rights!
For, these in evidence, you clearlier claim
A like garb for the rest, – grace all, the same
As these my peasants. (3:711–17)

This "shreds and patches" vision is Browning's version of the Carlylean phantasmagory – the sign which abjures "completeness" in order to be a genuine and motivated signifier. The symbol, for Browning, is therefore a "shred" returned to its synecdochic economy, like Venice: "'twixt blue and blue extends, a stripe, / As life, the somewhat, hangs 'twixt naught and naught" (3:724–5). The symbol, for Browning, is, in effect, what Dante is and what Sordello is not. Browning's purpose in *Sordello* is essentially that of Carlyle in *The French Revolution* – to separate the allegory from the symbol. In book 1, Browning calls Sordello the "forerunner" (1:348) of Dante, the "herald-star" (1:349) who has been relentlessly absorbed into the "consummate orb" (1:350) of Dante's influence and fame. What Browning proposes to do is "approach the august sphere / Named now with only one name" and "disentwine" (1:360–1) the silver undercurrents from "its fierce mate in the majestic mass" (1:363), now "[l]eavened as the sea whose fire was mixt with glass / In John's transcendent vision" (1:364–5); in short, he proposes to separate glass from fire, forerunner from genuine prophet. Like Carlyle's *The French Revolution*, Browning's *Sordello* is an attempt to transcend the economics of the word.

Conclusion

In *Dream Worlds: Mass Consumption in Late Nineteenth-Century France*, Rosalind H. Williams makes an explicit connection between the consumer revolution of the nineteenth century and events in French history. Citing the French aristocracy and its definition of "civilization" as the "prototype" of consumer habits, Williams makes a case for the "concept of *civilization*" as "an authoritative guide for the consumer ... by positing a humanistic idea capable of giving consumption a meaning and purpose." This guide, however, disintegrated towards the beginning of the nineteenth century when the "humanistic ideal of *civilization* tended to evaporate, leaving behind a residue of material possessions which by themselves claimed prestige for their owners. By the end of that century, the model of consumption that had originated in prerevolutionary court life had become degraded to the level of the heavy velour curtains, crystal chandeliers, ornate mirrors and imitation Louis xv divans in the cramped salons of aspiring tradesmen."[1] What is interesting about Williams's comment is her attribution to pre-revolutionary consumer goods of the "presence" of motivated signification. These were once valid symbols of French nobility and their presence guaranteed in some fashion the substance of civilization. In essence, these goods belonged to an economy of representation that gave the sign an authentic referentiality. In the Coleridgean symbol, the sign "partakes of the Reality which it renders intelligible"; the sign is therefore not merely a figure of speech or an abstracted name, but a material signifier that is "part" and "representative" of a "unity."[2] Consumer goods in themselves do not necessarily predicate the devouring imperatives of consumption. It is the dissolution of these consumer goods to mere signs, mere abstractions, that has created the proverbial "beast" of consumption. By the same token, it is the mass circulation of words as signs, as an accessible currency for a growing reading public, that has contributed to the problem of consumer texts. The alliance of economic viability and representation places language within a conventional and arbitrary system; as such, it poses an undeniable threat to the guardians of prophetic language, like Coleridge, who insists that words can never be arbitrary, for they are "Living Things."[3] Similarly, the economic motive behind Carlyle's use of Gothicism in *The French Revolution* is a deliberate stand against mass culture. The crisis of sovereignty implicit in the French Revolution is more than a question of national representation; it is a question of linguistic and aesthetic representation, and the choice posed before us is the legitimacy of representation by consensus or representation by merit. In representation by contract such as that espoused by Rousseau, strength indeed resides in numbers, and in this facile appropriation of right by consensus Carlyle sees the dangers of a "cash nexus" economy that is becoming standard in Victorian England. There is in the single-minded pursuit of money for money's sake a residual disharmony that Carlyle carries most aptly within a Gothic paradigm. The "monster" created by a logic of equivalence returns to "remonstrate," to chastise those who have created the imbalance which has effected its spawning. Both scourge and cure, Carlyle's Gothicism remains an inviolate means of revisioning language. If, through circulation, man is made mere "token" of genuine value, there are, perhaps, redemptive possibilities in an economy resistant to the economics of easy transference. Rejecting representation by number as an over-facile strategy of unity, Carlyle urges a more legitimate and authentic representation by merit; it is on the basis of this concept of legitimacy that Carlyle develops his Gothicism and deploys it within a specific author-reader relationship. Representation by merit unmasks the fiction of arbitrary representation. It returns the signifier to the signified by engendering confrontation and assimilation beyond the confines of consensus. It ensures that the act of representation exceeds its capacity as exchange to become a "total" act; if currency is based on a logic of exchange by which the thing is separated from the abstract value imposed on it, representation by merit would at least return thing to thought in a barter economy of expression. A brotherhood of literacy promises more than a "fit" audience; it is ultimately a vindication of linguistic and aesthetic prerogatives against the encroachment of mass consumption.

Notes

INTRODUCTION

1 Kaplan, *Thomas Carlyle*, 63.
2 Ibid., 192.
3 Ibid., 234.
4 Cumming, *Disimprisoned Epic*, 3.
5 Rosenberg, *Carlyle and the Burden of History*, 13.
6 Aristotle, *Politics*, 277.
7 Edmund Burke, *Reflections*, 94.
8 De Man, *Allegories of Reading*, 253.

CHAPTER ONE

1 Friedman, *Fabricating History*, 139.
2 Spector, intro. to *Seven Masterpieces*, 2.
3 Blake, *Complete Poetry and Prose*, 39.
4 Ibid., 42.
5 Ibid., 40.
6 In "Characteristics," Carlyle suggests a distinction between speculation and prophecy; the former is the "Thought" that "conducts not to the Deed; but in boundless chaos[,] self-devouring, engenders monstrosities, fantasms" (*W*, 28:28); the latter is "Speculation" that was "wholesome, for it ranged itself as the handmaid of Action" (*W*, 28:31). Prophecy is therefore speculation that leads to action while speculation itself is mere wishful thinking.

7 Schlegel, "On Incomprehensibility," 33–4.
8 Kant, *Prolegomena*, 7.
9 Schiller, *Works*, 5:6.
10 Schelling, "On the Study of Philosophy," 62.
11 Kenneth Burke, *Grammar of Motives*, 92.
12 Aristotle, *Politics*, 49.
13 Kenneth Burke, *Grammar of Motives*, 92.
14 Eagleton, *Literary Theory*, 166.
15 Smith, *Enquiry into the Wealth of Nations*, 1:34. Quotations are cited in the text. References are to volume and page.
16 Goux, *Symbolic Economies*, 123.
17 Ibid., 13.
18 Marc Shell, *Economy of Literature*, 55–6.
19 Marx, *Grundrisse*, 71. Quotations are cited in the text.
20 Rousseau, *Social Contract*, 64.
21 Coleridge, *Biographia Literaria*, 1:298. Quotations are cited in the text. References are to volume and page.
22 Sanders, *Carlyle's Friendships*, 45.
23 Harrold, *Carlyle and German Thought*, 54.
24 Ashton, *The German Idea*, 19.
25 Harrold, *Carlyle and German Thought*, 54; Ashton, *The German Idea*, 94.
26 Ashton, *The German Idea*, 46, 97.
27 Martin, intro. to Schelling, *The Unconditional in Human Knowledge*, 20.
28 I am using this word in the sense that Tzvetan Todorov uses it in *Theories of the Symbol*: utilitarian language is "referential, communicative and expressive," but intransitive language expresses only itself. Intransitive language is therefore an end in itself.
29 Ashton, *The German Idea*, 92.
30 Kant, *Critique of Pure Reason*, 24. Quotations are cited in the text.
31 The unconditional in human knowledge can be seen as the synecdochic extension of the conditional self; in this sense, it is intransitive as it remains an end (or a whole) in itself.
32 Susan Meld Shell, *Rights of Reason*, 80.
33 Ibid., 80, 81.
34 Kant, *Fundamental Principles*, 45.
35 In an earlier passage in *Fundamental Principles of the Metaphysics of Morals*, Kant writes: "The categorical imperative would be that which represented an action as necessary of itself without reference to another end, that is, as objectively necessary" (31).
36 Kant, *Fundamental Principles*, 50.
37 Kant, *Anthropology*, 39.
38 Ibid., 39.

39 Coleridge, *Complete Works*, 1:437. Quotations are cited in the text. References are to volume and page.
40 Hodgson, *Coleridge, Shelley and Transcendental Inquiry*, 3.
41 Foucault, "Order of Discourse," 69.
42 Edmund Burke, *Reflections*, 250. Quotations are cited in the text.
43 Foucault, "Order of Discourse," 50.

CHAPTER TWO

1 Hauhart, *Reception of Goethe's Faust*, 18–27.
2 Goethe, *Collected Works*. Quotations are cited in the text. References from part I and II of *Faust* are to volume and line.
3 Weisinger, *Classical Facade*, 27.
4 Goethe, *Collected Works*, 12:158. Quotations are cited in the text. Reference here is to volume and page.
5 John R. Williams, *Goethe's Faust*, 95–6.
6 Marc Shell, *Money, Language and Thought*, 87, 91–2.
7 According to Peter Conrad, in *The Everyman History of English Literature*, the Jonsonian masque is "the play as the ritualised unmasking of truth, and (when the sovereign is revealed) of power at its source" (198). This court masque takes a definite form; by dispelling the unholy and riotous elements of a preceding anti-masque, the masque serves to reinforce the royal prerogative. Goethe reverses the structure of the court masque: his royal pageantry is unmasked by violence.
8 Orgel, *Jonsonian Masque*, 19.
9 Lewis, *The Monk*, 44. Quotations are cited in the text.
10 Maturin, *Melmoth the Wanderer*, 212–3. Quotations are cited in the text.
11 Cumming, *Disimprisoned Epic*, 44.
12 Ibid.

CHAPTER THREE

1 Sartre, "Why Write?", 1060.
2 Ibid., 1062.
3 Rajan, *Supplement of Reading*, 29–30.
4 Ibid., 33.
5 Iser, *Act of Reading*, 108.
6 Ibid., 111.
7 Ibid., 115.
8 Ibid., 116.
9 Rajan, *Supplement of Reading*, 10.
10 Iser, *Act of Reading*, 180.

11 France, *Rhetoric and Truth in France*, 236. My translation: "I wish to be able in some fashion to render my soul transparent to the eyes of the reader."
12 Aarsleff, *From Locke to Saussure*, 38–9.
13 Coleridge, *Complete Works*, 1:218n. Quotations are cited in the text. References are to volume and page.
14 Coleridge, *Collected Letters*, 2:698. Reference is to volume and page.
15 McKusick, *Coleridge's Philosophy of Language*, 51.
16 Ibid., 50, 52.
17 Iser, *Act of Reading*, 186.
18 Woodman, *Addiction to Perfection*, 35, 29, 32
19 Ibid., 37.
20 Woodman, *Ravaged Bridegroom*, 92.
21 Woodman, *Addiction to Perfection*, 91.
22 Ibid., 91, 187.
23 Kenneth Burke, *Grammar of Motives*, 328, italics mine. Quotations are cited in the text.
24 Edmund Burke, *Reflections*, 110, 141.
25 Ibid., 94.
26 Foucault, "Order of Discourse," 69.
27 Blake, *Complete Poetry and Prose*, 39.
28 Rajan, *Supplement of Reading*, 2.
29 Cumming, *Disimprisoned Epic*, 69.

CHAPTER FOUR

1 De Man, *Allegories of Reading*, 253.
2 Marin, *Food for Thought*, 193–4. Quotations are cited in the text.
3 Rousseau, *Social Contract*, 105.
4 De Man, *Allegories of Reading*, 253. Quotations are cited in the text.
5 Rousseau, *Social Contract*, 55, 87.
6 Ibid., 63.

CHAPTER FIVE

1 Cumming, *Disimprisoned Epic*, 3–4.
2 Latané, *Browning's Sordello*, 22, 18.
3 Ibid., 20.
4 Browning, *Sordello*, 1:800–1. Quotations are cited in the text. References are to book and line.
5 Browning, *The Poems*, 1:150. Reference here is to volume and page.

CONCLUSION

1 Rosalind Williams, *Dream Worlds*, 8, 9.
2 Coleridge, *Complete Works*, 1:437, 438.
3 Coleridge, *Collected Letters*, 1:626.

Bibliography

Aarsleff, Hans. *From Locke to Saussure: Essays on the Study of Language and Intellectual History*. Minnesota: University of Minnesota Press, 1982.
Abrams, M.H. *Natural Supernaturalism: Tradition and Revolution in Romantic Literature*. New York: Norton, 1971.
Andersen, Roger. *The Power and the Word: Language, Power and Change*. London: Paladin, 1988.
Arac, Jonathan. *Commissioned Spirit: The Shape of Social Motion in Dickens, Carlyle, Melville and Hawthorne*. Brunswick: Rutgers University Press, 1979.
Aristotle. *The Politics*. Trans. Carnes Lord. Chicago: University of Chicago Press, 1984.
Ashton, Rosemary. *The German Idea: Four English Writers and the Reception of German Thought 1800–1860*. Cambridge: Cambridge University Press, 1980.
– "Carlyle's Apprenticeship: His Early German Criticism and his relationship with Goethe." *Modern Language Review* 71 (1976): 1–18.
Bahktin, Mikhail. *The Dialogic Imagination*. Ed. Michael Holquist. Trans. Caryl Emerson and Michael Holquist. Austin: University of Texas Press, 1981.
Baker, Keith M. *Inventing the French Revolution: Essays on French Political Culture in the Eighteenth Century*. Cambridge: Cambridge University Press, 1990.
Banfield, Ann. *Unspeakable Sentences: Narration and Representation in the Language of Fiction*. Boston: Routledge, 1982.
Barish, Jonas. *The Antitheatrical Prejudice*. Berkeley: University of California Press, 1981.
Bender, John. *Imagining the Penitentiary*. Chicago: University of Chicago Press, 1987.

Blake, William. *The Complete Poetry and Prose of William Blake*. Ed. David V. Erdman. Berkeley: University of California Press, 1982.

Bloomfield, Morton W., ed. *Allegory, Myth, and Symbol*. Harvard English Studies 9. Cambridge: Harvard University Press, 1981.

Boerner, Peter, and Sidney Johnson, eds. *Faust through Four Centuries: Retrospect and Analysis*. Tubingen: Verlag, 1989.

Boyle, Nicholas. "The Politics of *Faust II*: Another Look at the Stratum of 1831." *Publications of the English Goethe Society* 52 (1983): 4–43.

Brantlinger, Patrick. *The Spirit of Reform: British Literature and Politics, 1832–67*. Cambridge: Harvard University Press, 1977.

Browning, Robert. "Sordello." *The Poems*. Ed. John Pettigrew and Thomas J. Collins. 2 vols. Vol. 1. New Haven: Yale University Press, 1981. 149–296.

Burke, Edmund. "Reflections on the Revolution in France." *Reflections on the Revolution in France and the Rights of Man*. New York: Doubleday, 1961.

Burke, Kenneth. *A Grammar of Motives*. Berkeley: University of California Press, 1969.

Carlyle, Thomas. *The Collected Letters of Thomas and Jane Welsh Carlyle*. Ed. Charles Richard Sanders and Kenneth J. Fielding. 9 vols. Durham: Duke University Press, 1970–81.

– *The Correspondence of Carlyle and Emerson*. Ed. Charles Eliot Norton. 2 vols. London: Chatto, 1883.

– *The Works of Thomas Carlyle*. Centenary Ed. 30 vols. New York: AMS, 1969.

– *Two Note Books of Thomas Carlyle*. Ed. Charles Eliot Norton. 1989. Mamaroneck: Appel, 1972.

Castle, Terry. *Masquerade and Civilization: The Carnivalesque in Eighteenth Century Culture and Fiction*. Stanford: Stanford University Press, 1986.

Christ, Carol. *Victorian and Modern Poetics*. Chicago: University of Chicago Press, 1984.

Clark, Kenneth. *The Gothic Revival: An Essay in the History of Taste*. London: Penguin, 1964.

Cohn, Dorrit. *Transparent Minds: Narrative Modes for Presenting Consciousness in Fiction*. New Jersey: Princeton University Press, 1978.

Coleridge, Samuel T. *Biographia Literaria*. Ed. James Engell and W. Jackson Bate. 2 vols. Princeton: Princeton University Press, 1983.

– *Collected Letters of Samuel Taylor Coleridge*. Ed. Earl Leslie Gripps. 6 vols. Oxford: Clarendon, 1956.

– *The Complete Works of Samuel Taylor Coleridge*. Ed. W.G.T. Shedd. 7 vols. New York: Harper, 1884.

Comninel, George C. *Rethinking the French Revolution: Marxism and the Revisionist Challenge*. London: Verso, 1987.

Conger, Syndy M. *Matthew G. Lewis, Charles Robert Maturin and the Germans: An Interpretative Study of the Influence of German Literature in Two Gothic Novels*. New York: Arno Press, 1980.

Conrad, Peter. *The Everyman History of English Literature*. London: Dent, 1985.
Cottom, Daniel. *The Civilized Imagination: A Study of Ann Radcliffe, Jane Austen and Sir Walter Scott*. Cambridge: Cambridge University Press, 1985.
Crocker, Lester G. *Jean-Jacques Rousseau*. 2 vols. New York: Macmillan, 1977.
Cumming, Mark. *A Disimprisoned Epic*. Philadelphia: University of Pennsylvania Press, 1988.
Dale, Peter Allan. *The Victorian Critic and the Idea of History: Carlyle, Arnold, Pater*. Cambridge: Harvard University Press, 1979.
Danto, Arthur C. *The Transfiguration of the Commonplace: A Philosophy of Art*. Cambridge: Harvard University Press, 1981.
Day, William Patrick. *In the Circles of Fear and Desire: A Study of Gothic Fantasy*. Chicago: University of Chicago Press, 1985.
De Bolla, Peter. *The Discourse of the Sublime: Readings in History, Aesthetics and the Subject*. Oxford: Blackwell, 1989.
de Man, Paul. *Allegories of Reading: Figural Language in Rousseau, Nietzche, Rilke, and Proust*. New Haven: Yale University Press, 1979.
– "The Rhetoric of Temporality." *Blindness and Insight: Essays in the Rhetoric of Contemporary Criticism*. 1971. Minneapolis: University of Minnesota Press, 1983. 187–228.
Dowling, Linda. *Language and Decadence in the Victorian Fin de Siècle*. Princeton: Princeton University Press, 1986.
Eagleton, Terry. *Literary Theory*. Minneapolis: University of Minnesota Press, 1983.
Ermath, Elizabeth. *Realism and Consensus in the English Novel*. Princeton: Princeton University Press, 1983.
Essick, Robert N. *William Blake and the Language of Adam*. Oxford: Clarendon, 1989.
Evans, Robin. *The Fabrication of Virtue: English Prison Architecture 1750–1840*. Cambridge: Cambridge University Press, 1982.
Foucault, Michel. *Discipline and Punish: The Birth of the Prison*. Trans. Alan Sheridan. New York: Pantheon, 1977.
– *Power/Knowledge: Selected Interviews and Other Writings 1972–1977*. Ed. Colin Gordon. Trans. Colin Gordon et al. New York: Pantheon, 1980.
– "The Order of Discourse." *Untying the Text: A Post-Structuralist Reader*. Ed. Robert Young. Boston: Routledge, 1981.
France, Peter. *Rhetoric and Truth in France: Descartes to Diderot*. Oxford: Clarendon, 1972.
Frankl, Paul. *The Gothic: Literary Sources and Interpretation through Eight Centuries*. Princeton: Princeton University Press, 1960.
Fried, Michael. *Absorption and Theatricality: Painting and the Eye of the Beholder in the Age of Diderot*. Berkeley: University of California Press, 1980.
Friedman, Burton. *Fabricating History: English Writers on the French Revolution*. Princeton: Princeton University Press, 1988.

Frye, Northrop. *The Secular Scripture: A Study of the Structure of Romance.* Cambridge: Harvard University Press, 1976.
Gauthier, David. *Moral Dealing: Contract, Ethics, and Reason.* Ithaca: Cornell University Press, 1990.
Godwin, William. *Caleb Williams.* New York: Holt, 1960.
Goethe, Johann W. von. *Goethe's Collected Works.* Ed. and trans. Stuart Atkins. 12 vols. Cambridge: Suhrkamp/Insel, 1984.
Goux, Jean-Joseph. *Symbolic Economies.* Trans. Jennifer Curtiss Gage. Ithaca: Cornell University Press, 1990.
Graham, Kenneth W., ed. *Gothic Fictions: Prohibition/Transgression.* New York: AMS, 1989.
Haggarty, G.E. "Fact and Fancy in the Gothic Novel." *Nineteenth Century Fiction* 39 (1985): 379–41.
Harpham, Geoffrey G. *On the Grotesque: Strategies of Contradiction in Art and Literature.* Princeton: Princeton University Press, 1982.
Harrison, Ross. *Bentham.* London: Routledge, 1983.
Harrold, Charles Frederick. *Carlyle and German Thought 1819–1834.* New York: AMS, 1978.
Hauhart, William. F. *The Reception of Goethe's Faust in England in the First Half of the Nineteenth Century.* 1909. New York: AMS, 1966.
Henley, Keith, and Roman Selden, eds. *Revolution and English Romanticism.* New York: St Martin's, 1990.
Hodgson, John A. *Coleridge, Shelley and Transcendental Inquiry.* Lincoln: University of Nebraska Press, 1989.
Ignatieff, Michael. *A Just Measure of Pain: The Penitentiary in the Industrial Revolution 1750–1850.* Harmondsworth: Penguin, 1978.
– *The Needs of Strangers: An Essay on Privacy, Solidarity and the Politics of Being Human.* Harmondsworth: Penguin, 1984.
Iser, Wolfgang. *The Act of Reading: A Theory of Aesthetic Response.* Baltimore: Johns Hopkins University Press, 1978.
Jameson, Fredric. *The Political Unconscious: Narrative as a Socially Symbolic Act.* Ithaca: Cornell University Press, 1981.
– *The Prison-House of Language: A Critical Account of Structuralism and Russian Formalism.* Princeton: Princeton University Press, 1974.
Kant, Immanuel. *Anthropology from a Practical Point of View.* Ed. Hans. H. Rudnick. Trans. Victor Lyle Dowdell. Carbondale: Southern Illinois University Press, 1978.
– *Fundamental Principles of the Metaphysics of Morals.* Trans. Thomas K. Abbott. Indianapolis: Bobbs, 1949.
– *Prolegomena to Any Future Metaphysics.* Ed. Lewis White Beck. New York: Bobbs, 1950.
– *Critique of Pure Reason.* Trans. Norman Kemp Smith. New York: St Martin's, 1965.

Kaplan, Fred. *Thomas Carlyle: A Biography*. Ithaca: Cornell University Press, 1983.
– *Thomas Carlyle: A Biography*. Ithaca: Cornell University Press, 1983.
Kayser, Wolfgang. *The Grotesque in Art and Literature*. Trans. Ulrich Weisstein. New York: Columbia, 1963.
Kliger, Samuel. *The Goths in England: A Study in Seventeenth and Eighteenth Century Thought*. Cambridge: Harvard University Press, 1952.
Knapp, Steven. *Personification and the Sublime: Milton to Coleridge*. Cambridge: Harvard University Press, 1985.
Latané, David E. *Browning's "Sordello" and the Aesthetics of Difficulty*. Victoria: University of Victoria Press, 1987.
LaValley, Albert J. *Carlyle and the Idea of the Modern*. New Haven: Yale University Press, 1968.
Leicester, H.M. "The Dialectic of Romantic Historiography: Prospect and Retrospect in *The French Revolution*." *Victorian Studies* 15 (1971): 5–17.
Levine, George. *The Realistic Imagination: English Fiction From "Frankenstein" to "Lady Chatterley"*. Chicago: University of Chicago Press, 1981.
Lewis, Matthew. *The Monk*. New York: Grove, 1952.
MacAndew, Elizabeth. *The Gothic Tradition in Fiction*. New York: Columbia University Press, 1979.
Malins, Edward. *English Landscaping and Literature 1660–1840*. London: Oxford University Press, 1966.
Marin, Louis. *Food for Thought*. Baltimore: Johns Hopkins University Press, 1989.
Martin, Fritz. Introduction to Schelling, *The Unconditional in Human Knowledge*. Lewisburg: Bucknell University Press, 1980. 17–28.
Marx, Karl. *Grundrisse*. Ed. and trans. David McLellan. London: Macmillan, 1971.
Maturin, Charles. *Melmoth the Wanderer*. Ed. Douglas Grant. Oxford: Oxford University Press, 1989.
McKusick, James C. *Coleridge's Philosophy of Language*. New Haven: Yale University Press, 1986.
Mellor, Anne K. *English Romantic Irony*. Cambridge: Harvard University Press, 1980.
Molnár, Géza von. "The Conditions of Faust's Wager and Its Resolution in the Light of Kantian Ethics." *Publications of the English Goethe Society* 51 (1981): 48–80.
Nisbet, H.B. *German Aesthetic and Literary Criticism: Winckelmann, Lessing, Hamann, Herder, Schiller, Goethe*. Cambridge: Cambridge University Press, 1985.
Orgel, Stephen. *The Jonsonian Masque*. Cambridge: Harvard University Press, 1965.
Paradic, James and Thomas Postlewait, eds. *Victorian Science and Victorian Values: Literary Perspectives*. Brunswick: Rutgers University Press, 1985.

Paulson, Ronald. *Representations of Revolution*. New Haven: Yale University Press, 1983.

Pocock, J.G.A. *Virtue, Commerce and History: Essays on Political Thought and History, Chiefly in the Eighteenth Century*. Cambridge: Cambridge University Press, 1985.

Punter, David. *The Literature of Terror: A History of Gothic Conventions from 1765 to the Present Day*. London: Longman, 1980.

Rajan, Tilottama. *The Supplement of Reading: Figures of Understanding in Romantic Theory and Practice*. Ithaca: Cornell University Press, 1990.

Raphael, D. "The Impartial Spectator." *Essays on Adam Smith*. Ed. Andrew S. Skinner and Thomas Wilson. Oxford: Clarendon, 1975. 83–99.

Ritter, Allan, and Julia Conaway Bondanella, eds. *Rousseau's Political Writings*. Trans. Julia Conaway Bondanella. New York: Norton, 1988.

Ronald, Ann. *Functions of Setting in the Novel from Mrs. Radcliffe to Charles Dickens*. New York: Arno Press, 1980.

Rosenberg, John D. *Carlyle and the Burden of History*. Cambridge: Harvard University Press, 1985.

Rosenberg, Philip. *The Seventh Hero: Thomas Carlyle and the Theory of Radical Activism*. Cambridge: Harvard University Press, 1974.

Rousseau, Jean-Jacques. *The Social Contract*. Trans. Maurice Cranston. Harmondsworth: Penguin, 1968.

– *A Discourse on Inequality*. Trans. Maurice Cranston. Harmondsworth: Penguin, 1984.

Ryan, Alan. *Property and Political Theory*. Oxford: Blackwell, 1984.

Sanders, Charles R. *The Carlyle-Browning Correspondence and Relationship*. Manchester: John Rylands University Library, 1975.

– *Carlyle's Friendships and Other Studies*. Durham: Duke University Press, 1977.

Sartre, Jean-Paul. "Why Write?" *Critical Theory since Plato*. Ed. Hazard Adams. Trans. Bernard Frechtman. Toronto: Harcourt, 1971.

Schelling, F.W.J. "On the Study of Philosophy." *On University Studies*. Ed. Norbert Guterman. Trans. E.S. Morgan. Athens: Ohio University Press, 1966. 609–70.

Schiller, Friedrich. *Works of Schiller*. Ed. Nathan Haskell Dole. 5 vols. Boston: C.T. Brainard, 1902.

Schlegel, Frederick. "An Essay on Gothic Architecture." *Aesthetics and Miscellaneous Works of Frederick von Schlegel*. Trans. and ed. E.J. Millington. London: Bohn, 1860.

– *Dialogue on Poetry and Literary Aphorisms*. Trans. and ed. Ernst Behler and Roman Struc. University Park: Pennsylvania State University Press, 1908.

– "On Incomprehensibility." *German Aesthetics and Literary Criticism: The Romantic Ironists and Goethe*. Ed. Kathleen M. Wheeler. London: Cambridge University Press, 1984. 32–39.

Shell, Marc. *The Economy of Literature*. Baltimore: Johns Hopkins University Press, 1978.
- *Money, Language and Thought: Literary and Philosophical Economies from the Medieval to the Modern Era*. Berkeley: University of California Press, 1982.
Shell, Susan Meld. *The Rights of Reason: A Study of Kant's Philosophy and Politics*. Toronto: University of Toronto Press, 1980.
Smith, Adam. *An Enquiry into the Wealth of Nations*. Ed. Edwin Canaan. 2 vols. Chicago: University of Chicago Press, 1976.
Smith, Warren Hunting. *Architecture in English Fiction*. New Haven: Yale University Press, 1934.
Spector, Donald. Introduction. *Seven Masterpieces of Gothic Horror*. Ed. Donald Spector. New York: Bantam, 1983. 1–11.
- *The English Gothic: A Bibliographic Guide to Writers from Horace Walpole to Mary Shelley*. Westport, Conn.: Greenwood Press, 1984.
Thompson, G.R., ed. *The Gothic Imagination: Essays on Dark Romanticism*. Pullman: Washington State University Press, 1974.
Todorov, Tzvetan. *The Fantastic: A Structural Approach to a Literary Genre*. Trans. Richard Howard. Ithaca: Cornell University Press, 1975.
- *Theories of the Symbol*. Trans. Catherine Porter. Ithaca: Cornell University Press, 1977.
Turner, Brian S. *Citizenship and Capitalism: The Debate over Reformism*. London: Allen, 1986.
Vernon, Richard. *Citizenship and Order: Studies in French Political Thought*. Toronto: University of Toronto Press, 1986.
Walpole, Horace. *The Castle of Otranto: A Gothic Story*. Ed. W.S. Lewis. London: Oxford University Press, 1969.
Weisinger, Kenneth D. *The Classical Façade: A Nonclassical Reading of Goethe's Classicism*. University Park: Pennsylvania State University Press, 1988.
Weiss, Frederick. *The Antispectre: Satire in Early Gothic Novels*. New York: Arno Press, 1980.
Wellbery, David E. *Lessing's Laocoön: Semiotics and Aesthetics in the Age of Reason*. Cambridge: Cambridge University Press, 1984.
Wheeler, Kathleen. *German Aesthetics and Literary Criticism: The Romantic Ironists and Goethe*. Cambridge: Cambridge University Press, 1984.
White, Allon. *The Uses of Obscurity: The Fiction of Early Modernism*. London: Routledge, 1981.
Williams, John R. *Goethe's Faust*. London: Allen, 1987.
Williams, Rosalind. *Dream Worlds: Mass Consumption in Late Nineteenth-Century France*. Berkeley: University of California Press, 1982.
Woodman, Marion. *Addiction to Perfection*. Toronto: Inner City, 1982.
- *The Ravaged Bridegroom*. Toronto: Inner City, 1990.

Index

Aarsleff, Hans: *From Locke to Saussure*, 67
aesthetics of incomprehensibility, 4–5, 11–12, 13, 105–6
Aids to Reflection (Coleridge), 24–8
Allegories of Reading (de Man), 94, 100–4
allegory and symbol: in Browning, 107–11, 119; in Carlyle, 8, 24, 29–30, 32–3, 36, 102–3, 119, 120–1; in Coleridge, 6, 24–30, 120–1; in Goethe, 36, 39–49
Anthropology from a Practical Point of View (Kant), 23nn37–8
Aristotle: *The Politics*, 12
Ashton, Rosemary: *The German Idea*, 18

Biographia Literaria (Coleridge), 17–18, 21, 24, 26, 28–9, 63–4
Blake, William, 11, 54, 115
body: and convalescence, 3–5, 4–6, 94, 98–9, 103–4; pathetic, 96–8, 100; politic, 7, 94–6, 98–102; as representation, 106–7; as symbol, 95; and text, 4–8, 94, 99
Browning, Robert, 8; and *Sordello*, 105–19
Burke, Edmund: *Reflections on the Revolution in France*, 30–3, 90
Burke, Kenneth: *A Grammar of Motives*, 12, 82–3

Carlyle, Lady Jane Welsh, 4
Carlyle, Thomas: aesthetic of incomprehensibility, 4–5, 11–12; allegory and symbol in works, 8, 24, 29–30, 32–3, 36, 102–3, 119, 120–1; and Blake, 10–11; and Coleridge, 6–7, 18, 69; and convalescence, 3–5, 13 (*see also* body); and Gothicism, 9–11, 30, 36, 47–8, 51–2, 56–9, 78–9, 121; and Kant, 18–20; and money, 5–6, 15, 17, 32–3, 91; and the third term, 6–7, 17–19; and transcendental philosophy, 6, 17–18
– *The French Revolution*: allegory and symbol in, 6–7, 29, 69–73, 75–8, 81, 85–6, 90–3, 102–4, 119; anomaly in style, 8–9; body and text in, 94, 99–100; the Constitution in, 83, 88–90; economics and economy in, 7–8, 92–3, 103; epic machinery in, 71–2, 76, 86–7; the eucharist in, 79–82; fragmenting devices in, 70–1; Gothicism in, 5–9, 59–60, 69–70, 74, 75, 78–9, 81–7, 88–96; the hero in, 93, 102–3; the masque in, 48, 55–6, 73, 84–5; and mass culture, 120–1; Napoleon in, 69, 75, 76, 77, 102; paper age in, 16–17, 73–4; phantasmagory in, 9, 90; philosophism

in, 73–8; the procession in, 69–72; as response to Burke, 7, 32–3, 90; and reading, 7–8, 64–8, 70, 74–8, 83–4, 88–9, 90, 92–3, 102; real and logical oppositions in, 90–1; and *The Social Contract*, 13, 16, 60–1, 64, 66–7, 100–3; and *Sordello*, 8, 105, 107, 119; and the third term, 81
– Other Works: "Characteristics," 13, 15, 103–4; "The Diamond Necklace," 35, 57–63; "Goethe," 11; Goethe's Helena," 36–7; "Goethe's Works," 37; "The Hero as a Man of Letters," 16; "On History," 66; *Past and Present*, 5–6; *Sartor Resartus*, 15, 29; "State of German Literature," 11–12; "Taylor's Historic Survey of German Literature," 10
Castle of Otranto (Walpole), 10
Coleridge, S.T.: allegory and symbol, 6, 24–30, 81, 120–1; on common sense, 26; on language and money, 28; and logical and real oppositions, 17–18, 27, 39; on the Noetic Pentad, 68–102; on synonimization, 25–6; theory of language, 68–9, 121; and the third term, 6–7, 17–18, 63, 81
– Works: *Aids to Reflection*, 24–8; *Biographia Literaria*, 24, 26, 28–9, 63–4
Constitution, the, 6–7, 66–7, 83–90
Cumming, Mark: *A Disimprisoned Epic*, 9, 56–7, 93

de Man, Paul: *Allegories of Reading*, 94, 100–4; metaphors of totalization, 8, 94, 100

Eagleton, Terry: *Literary Theory*, 13
economics: barter vs money economies, 14–15; and economy 6–7, 12–13, 103; and language, 3–6, 9–13, 23–9, 44–5, 90–1, 106, 120–1
economy: in Aristotle, 6; of Nature, in Goethe, 38–9
epic, 71, 75–7

Faust (Goethe): allegory and symbol in, 39–49; as criticism of classicism, 50–1; economic motifs in, 37–8, 43–7; the masque in, 44, 47–8, 48n7, 55–6; Mephistopheles in, 38–43, 48–9, 50–1; and phantasmagory, 45–6; reception in Britain, 34; and the third term, 39, 44–51; the wager in, 35–6, 47
Foucault, Michel: "Order of Discourse," 29, 32–3
French Revolution, The: see entry under Carlyle
Friedman, Burton: *Fabricating History*, 9
Fundamental Principles of the Metaphysics of Morals (Kant), 23nn34–6

Goethe: allegory and symbol, 36, 39–43; on the economy of Nature, 38–9; as ideal reader, 62, 92–3; on money and language, 44
– Works: "Faust," 34–56; "Polarity," 38–9;

"Symbolism," 44; "Theory of Colour," 38–9
Gothicism, 5–7, 9–11, 33, 34–5; *see also* Gothic romances
Gothic romances, 7, 10
Goux, Jean-Joseph: *Symbolic Economies*, 14
Grundrisse (Marx), 15–16

Harrold, Charles Frederick: *Carlyle and German Thought*, 18
Hodgson, John A.: *Coleridge, Shelley and Transcendental Inquiry*, 24

Iser, Wolfgang: *The Act of Reading*, 63, 66

Kant, Immanuel: and Adam Smith, 22–3; and common sense, 12; and logical opposition, 21; money and metaphysics, 20–1, 22–4; and the third term, 17–21
– Works: *Anthropology from a Practical Point of View*, 23nn37–8; *Fundamental Principles of the Metaphysics of Morals*, 23nn34–6; Preface to the second edition of *The Critique of Pure Reason*, 19–21; *Prolegomena to Any Future Metaphysics*, 12
Kaplan, Fred: *Thomas Carlyle*, 3–4

Latané, David: *Browning's "Sordello" and the Aesthetics of Difficulty*, 105
Lewis, Matthew: *The Monk*, 34–5, 54–6
logic of general equivalence: and Burke, 32–3; and Coleridge, 24–8; in

Index

Faust, 43–4, 47–51, 52–6; in *The French Revolution*, 62, 71, 76, 80–1, 86–7, 89; in Marx, 15–16; in Rousseau, 16–17; in *Sordello*, 115

McKusick, James C.: *Coleridge's Theory of Language*, 69
Mammonism, 4–5
Marin, Louis, 8; *Food for Thought*, 94–9
Marx, Karl: *Grundrisse*, 15–16; on money, 15–16
Maturin, Charles: *Melmoth the Wanderer*, 34–5, 53–6
mass culture: and language, 9–14, 26–9, 89–90, 109–10, 120–1
Melmoth the Wanderer (Maturin): and allegory, 54–6; and betrayal, 34–5; Catholicism and equivalence, 54–5; use of masque in, 55–6
Mill, John Stuart, 3
Monk, The (Lewis): and betrayal, 34–5; use of masque in, 52–3; monasticism, 52–3

"On the Study of Philosophy" (Schelling), 12
Orgel, Stephen: *The Jonsonian Masque*, 48

"Polarity" (Goethe), 38–9
Preface to the second edition of *The Critique of Pure Reason* (Kant), 19–21
Prolegomena to Any Future Metaphysics (Kant), 12

Rajan, Tilottama: *The Supplement of Reading*, 62
reading: and betrayal, 6, 34–5; and community, 7, 61–5, 91, 105; and the Constitution, 7, 66–7, 83–90; and economic metaphor, 7, 35; and logical opposition, 62–3; and mass culture, 120–1; prophetic and passive readers, 60–1, 63–4, 72–3, 109–10, 115–17; and prophetic language, 67–8; reader as hero, 93; reader as supplement, 7, 62, 92, 116–19; and select readership, 8, 105; and the third term, 62–3
Reflections on the Revolution in France (Burke), 7, 30–3, 90
representation: and community, 8, 16, 61–2, 80–90, 100–1, 121; and mass culture, 9–14, 26–9, 86–90, 109–110, 120–1; and sovereignty, 29–30, 96–9, 103
Richter, Jean Paul, 13
Rosenberg, John D., 5
Rousseau, Jean-Jacques: *The Social Contract*, 16, 60, 66–7, 94, 100–3; and transparency, 66–7

Sanders, Charles Richard: *The Carlyle-Browning Correspondence and Relationship*, 18
Sartre, Jean-Paul: "Why Write?", 61–2
Schelling, F.W.J., 19; "On the Study of Philosophy," 12
Schiller, Friedrich, 12
Schlegel, Frederick, 11
Shell, Marc: *The Economy of Literature*, 14–15; *Money, Language and Thought*, 44
Shell, Susan Meld: *The Rights of Reason*, 22–3
sign: as allegory, 24–9, 31–3, 39–49, 54–9, 69–78, 82–90, 94–6, 102–4, 108–11, 120–1 (*see also* allegory and symbol); as community, 82–90, 114–16; as convalescence, 98–9 (*see also* body); as logical opposition, 21–4, 27–9, 39–40, 95; as symbol, 24–33, 39–49, 62, 69–78, 82–96, 102–4, 111–15, 120–1; as the third term, 6–7, 17–21, 39, 44–51, 62–3, 113–14
Smith, Adam: *Enquiry into the Wealth of Nations*, 13–14, 21–3; and Kant, 22–3; on labour and exchange, 13–14, 22; on money and abstraction, 14; on paper currency, 21–3; on real and nominal prices, 14
Social Contract, The (Rousseau): as general equivalent, 16; as misreading, 94, 100–3; as wager, 66–7
Sordello (Browning): and allegory, 107–11, 115; brother's speech in, 105, 113–14; community in, 111–12; and currency, 109–10; 114–15; the masque in, 117–18; prophetic reader in, 105, 110; real opposition in, 109; the third term in, 111–13, 116
sovereignty: and representation, 7–8, 30–3, 47–8, 57–9, 65–8, 71–3, 90, 94–6, 99–104, 106, 114
Symbolic Economies (Goux), 14
"Symbolism" (Goethe), 44

terror: and economics, 5–6; in *Faust*, 48–9; in

Gothic romances, 34–5, 52–3, 55–6; and the Reign of Terror, 78–80, 88–90
tertium aliquid, 17–18; see also the third term
"Theory of Colour" (Goethe), 38–9
third term, the: and Carlyle, 6–7, 17–19; and Coleridge, 6–7, 17–18, 63, 81; in *Faust*, 39, 44–51; and Kant, 17–21; and reading, 62–3; in *Sordello*, 111–13, 116

wager, the, 7–8; in "The Diamond Necklace," 57–9, 60–1; in *Faust*, 34–7; in *The French Revolution*, 66–7, 73, 77, 83–5, 88–9; in Gothic romances, 34–5; in *Melmoth the Wanderer*, 53–5; in *The Monk*, 52–3
Walpole, Horace: *The Castle of Otranto*, 10

Wedgwood, Frances, 4
"Why Write?" (Sartre), 61–2
Williams, John R.: *Goethe's Faust*, 41–2
Williams, Rosalind: *Dream Worlds*, 120
Woodman, Marion: *Addiction to Perfection*, 80–1; on consumption and communion, 80–1; *The Ravaged Bridegroom*, 80–1